The right tool 1

I know a lot of people sigh about
frankly jobs are so much easier v
This was driven home to me today. We had a lamb that
was walking stiffly, didn't look 'right.' I noticed this when I
was feeding the batch of relatively newly lambed ewes and
their lambs out in the field.

So I tried to catch it. How difficult can it be; there was me
and Sal? I would provide the brains, and Sal could do the
Border Collie bit. Except that Sal knows fine well that when
lambs are this young, mothers are awfully protective. So
whilst she did run around a lot, she made damned sure she
never got close enough to offend anybody.

And the lamb, whilst stiff and slow, seemed to loosen up
the more it moved. The same might be true of me, but
we're working from different base-lines and it was always
going to be faster than me.

So I went back with no dog, the quad and a leg crook. I
followed the lamb and when it stopped to work out which
way to run next, I hooked the crook around its leg and
before it could work out what had happened I had slipped
off the quad, grabbed it and put it in the trailer.

Anyway examined at home we could see the 'wrists' were
thicker than you'd expect, it had probably picked up an
infection from somewhere, so we treated it and I took it
back to mum so she didn't forget it.

Then in the early afternoon I had to help at an interment of
ashes. (I'm the one that digs the hole. I know my place.)
People talk about 'scattering ashes.' Really you shouldn't,
they can contain far too high a proportion of phosphates
and heavy metals. So you inter them, or bury them. Over
the time I've been doing this, I've learned the hard way
what I need. A spade, (obviously) but ideally it's a decent
square ended spade that is about eight inches wide. Not
too flimsy, you might have to go through the smaller tree
roots you get at this sort of depth.

You need a long bar, like a crow-bar because some churchyard soils are stony and compacted, so the bar makes things so much easier. Then you want a plastic bag to put the sod on and two decent sized plastic buckets to put the soil into. If you have the right tackle to hand the job is easier and, especially important when you're working in a graveyard, it's easy to keep it tidy as well.

Finally I took advantage of the fine weather and walked to the village craft fair. I was talking to the lass who was organising it and it must be said I was entirely impressed with the apron she'd made herself. Take a pair of men's jeans, (Because they've got pockets at the back.) Then you cut away the legs so you are left with the bit from crotch to belt. Now I suppose you could have it as a skirt, but what she did was cut away the crotch at the front and then wore it 'back to front' as an apron but with all these useful pockets handy where she could see them.

I suppose one thing that you'd have to be careful about was getting the discarded jeans from an active male, not the sort that just wears out the seat of his pants first.

Ride a white swan

The maiden wasn't in distress as such, and she was probably a fair bit older than the fairytale ideal. But she obviously cared, which means a lot. Not only that, she didn't just care in the "click 'like' on Facebook with crying face emoji" sort of way. So she got on and did the job. But I suppose I'd better tell the tale in some sort of order.

I was just walking on my way from somewhere heading for somewhere else. I was just getting from one part of town to another to be honest. Time wasn't particularly pressing, but it was probably going to rain so I wasn't dawdling. Anyway, for no particular reason I took the path along the side of the reservoir.

Said "Hi" to the fishermen who were a bit fed up from the noise coming from a bunch of kids gathered round the back of a bar on the other side of the reservoir, picked my way along the muddy bits of the path and then came upon a lady, with a dog, who was feeding the swans.

So I said 'hi' to the dog as I normally do when they bound across to say 'hi' to me. It seems rude not to and once they've been acknowledged they'll often bound off to look at something more interesting. But this led to saying 'hi' to the owner.

Now this conversation was taking place against a background of swans, one of whom wasn't walking right. The maiden not actually in distress gestured to it and explained it had had some fishing line caught round its leg. She'd cut the fishing weight off with nail scissors but the line was still caught.

I asked, "Have you contacted the RSPCA."

"Yes, a fortnight ago. They said they couldn't do anything."

So she'd taken to feeding the swans, and after two weeks she'd plucked up the courage to go near enough to cut the trailing fishing weight off.

But it was obvious the rest of the line was still entangled. Now given she'd cut the weight off, it struck me that she was obviously used to handling them, so I suggested that, because it knew her, the swan would let her catch it, and then we could get the line off its leg.

At this point I might interrupt myself to rant about health and safety. People talk about how dangerous swans are. Trust me; they're smaller, lighter and less dangerous than cattle. Not only that but at the time, I was standing three feet from several of them and they didn't seem to regard me as a problem. End of rant.

So together we caught it, which was as simple as her putting her hands down and gently enfolding it in her arms whilst ensuring she held the top of its neck. I looked at the line, couldn't untangle it but luckily I cut it with a door key. Three minutes later we'd got rid of all traces of the line and the swan was back in the water and swimming off.

At this point a young couple with four children, a dog, and a bag of bread arrived. Husband asks if it was the swan with the tangled foot. Maiden no longer in distress explained it was and a discussion ensues.

At which point Maiden comments, "Until he asked me to, I'd never so much as touched a swan in my life."
(Apparently when cutting off the weight she'd crawled up to it on hands and knees.)
Anyway, all I can say to that is 'The lass done good.'
Anyway I made my farewells and left them all chatting happily, watching the swan swim away in the distance.
But it's nice to know that there are people who care, and not only who care, but care enough to crawl through the dirt on their hands and knees, equipped only with a pair of nail scissors, to do what they feel has to be done.
And still have the self-belief necessary to blithely pick up an adult swan when some wandering idiot asks you to, because it needs doing.
And as for the swan? Well it's got two chances, same as the rest of us. It'll either live or it'll die. Mind you, it would have a better chance of living if somebody had come out of the office and had done the job a fortnight ago.

The fast that I have chosen

I've spent the last forty-eight hours pondering social media. To be honest all I'd achieved is a growing level of despair, until I had a moment of revelation.
Instead of giving up stuff and fasting for Lent, I'd say the way forward is to give up stuff and fast for the election campaign!
So it struck me that I'd give up political discussions on social media. If a real person raises the topic when we are met together over a drink then that is fair enough, but no political discussions on social media. There are several reasons for this. Firstly they're a total waste of time, effort and electrons. (The latter could be better used elsewhere.)
Secondly the whole reason I started this social media stuff was because, sadly, I have books to sell. Screaming at somebody that they're the spawn of Satan because they're going to vote for the 'wrong' party doesn't strike me as one

of the better sales techniques. Well at least I've not had a lot of success with it so far.

Finally, life is too short to get wound up over arguments with people you'll never meet and care little for.

So far, and it's early days, things are going well. I've just avoided stuff. Indeed I have been a little cunning. I've not had to block anybody yet. But where they've merely shared a post by 'Sad politically obsessed loonies.com' I've blocked that page.

After all I don't mind people I know having opinions, but be damned if I'm wasting my time over websites created by political parties and their HQ black propaganda teams in an attempt to sway people to their way of thinking.

Now obviously I'm not going to be hard hearted about this. If 'Sad politically obsessed loonies.com' ever showed any signs of trying to relate to me, engage me in discussions about matters of importance in the real world, then I'd be more open to them.

Obviously this demands a change of track from them. Their normal output tends to be 'Our glorious party is composed entirely of persons who give their income to the poor, kiss the sores of lepers clean, and help infirm persons of all ages, genders and ethnicities across the road; while the other lot eat babies, sacrifice kittens to the dark gods of their ideology and if they win, then this is the last election you'll ever have.'

Personally I suggest that they post something along the lines of, "We believe that it is vitally important for the economy that people support our creative industries; thus we both urge and exhort you to purchase Jim Webster's fine story, 'Keeping Body and Soul Together'.

Should they do this I would certainly re-evaluate my approach. Not perhaps enough to vote for them, but certainly I'd give serious consideration to unblocking them on facebook.

Indeed if they were to go so far as to promise that in their efforts to improve literacy they would purchase a paperback copy of 'Swords for a Dead Lady' for every household, then I'd not merely no longer block them, I might even be prevailed upon to share their posts.

Still when I stop to think about it, there may indeed unforeseen advantages to my policy. By eschewing politics my facebook wall will become a place of peace and joy. Let others turn their social media shop window into a battleground for crazed warring factions, with barely literate political nonentities spluttering marginally coherent insults at each other.
My Facebook wall will be a tranquil oasis, tempting the war-weary traveller to rest awhile, allow the bitter anxiety to drain from them, and perhaps even relax into a good book that takes them away for the insanity that rages in less salubrious areas.

Which side is your bread buttered

It's amazing how rapidly moral principle can be overcome with simple greed. In a morning I go to feed sheep. I drive into the field on a quad bike towing a trailer and accompanied by Sal. Sal, as a border collie, has the silhouette of a small wolf and dentition any of the Canidae would be happy with. If sheep have in instinctive photofit of the apex predator to beware of, it's got Sal's paw prints all over it.
So the first time I do this we see sheep moving off at speed surrounded by their lambs. The second time I do it, some of the smarter ones have realised what I'm there for. By the end of the week they'll tread Sal (and me) underfoot to get to the feed first.
It's the same with the lambs. When you drive into the field, there'll be a ewe grazing quietly. She'll look up and bleat and her lambs will slowly disengage themselves from whatever they're doing and make their way to join her.

All except for the lambs of Number 39. Number 39 had triplets. Now normally we take one lamb off and give it to a ewe who just had a single. This is because a ewe only has two teats, and even without this issue, frankly struggles to produce enough milk to feed three lambs. In the case of Number 39 there was a run of triplets and she was the one giving the most milk so she was left with hers.

So whereas other lambs wander off to do strange and interesting things, Number 39's lambs stick with her, so they're first at the teat should they feel a tad peckish.

Mind you it's not something that is limited to sheep. My late mother and her two younger sisters would be invited to parties (we're talking before the war here.) And hostesses were always touched and delighted by the way the two younger sisters wanted to sit next to their big sister. This was always pointed out as a charming example of sisterly love.

In reality the reason was that my mother never liked marzipan or almond paste. So whenever we had fruitcake with icing on it, she (even in her seventies) would quietly slip her icing and marzipan to her neighbour. Her two little sisters were just making damned sure that when that happened, they were going to be the recipients.

Just follow the money!

Now it has to be confessed that I have a real ability to somehow get myself tangled up in dying industries. Look at agriculture. I know one year in the 1990s I discovered I'd been working over seventy hours a week at the princely rate of 9p an hour. But thanks to the internet, freelance journalism is going the same way.

When I'm doing proper freelance journalism, serious articles for trade papers, I reckon on getting £200 per thousand words, or 20p per word. For our American cousins that's about 26 cents a word.

For that you get a competent, literate and knowledgeable professional whose article will not merely be a rehash of wiki. As part of gathering the information I'll probably end up phoning and talking to people just to make sure what I'm saying is absolutely up-to-date and as right as I can make it.

Anyway as a freelance you're always looking for new work. Editors leave, magazines are sold, bought, disappear owing you serious money. Trust me in this, being a freelance isn't what I'd call a steady source of money.

So when I saw a website called 'Custom Content' offering freelance work I took a look. Their idea isn't bad, they act as a clearing house, but unusually they don't exist to put writer and client in contact, they have writers deliver content to the client via the website. Also the writer has to use a pen name so the client never really knows who it is who has done the work for them, and therefore cannot 'poach' them to do more work without paying an intermediary.

So what did this site pay their writers?

Well there are four grades of work.

The idea seems to be you start off on the lowest grade and as you collect more work and your clients seem happy you get promoted to higher grades.

 What the writer gets per word

1 Star: 1.2 cents
2 Star: 2.0 cents
3 Star: 4.4 cents
4 Star: 6.6 cents

Tweets and facebook posts are priced differently.

So having looked at what I, as a writer would be paid, I then looked at what I would have to pay if I decided to be a customer. Here they have the same four grades but with somewhat different names

What the client pays

Entry level   2.2 cents
Freelance   3.5 cents
Professional   8 cents
Expert   12 cents

 Just out of curiosity, how much was our website making on this? What's their cut? Simple arithmetic comes to our aid.

Company share per word
1 Star: -   1 cents
2 Star: -   1.5 cents
3 Star: -   3.6 cents
4 Star: -   5.4 cents

So for providing their service they were taking nearly half the money the customer was paying. Good work if you can get it.
So let's put this is perspective. Firstly I'm looking for 26 cents a word. That obviously puts me well out in front of their expert category.
So what are you getting for your money as a customer?
I mean, for 1 cent a word you can hardly expect somebody to check their spelling after hastily rewording the wiki article for you!

But we can also put things in a historical context. In 'Astounding Wonder: Imagining Science and Science Fiction in Interwar America,' written by John Cheng he discusses the old pulp magazines. In the 1920s writers were paid between 2 cents and 5 cents a word with one publisher of 'Westerns' paying 10 cents a word. Rates dropped a bit during the Great Depression, but still the comparison doesn't exactly flatter. 'Custom Content' is paying writers less than they would have earned in the 1920s.

They are assuming that writers can cope with a rate of pay that hasn't changed in a century! According to one web page, $100 in 1920 has the spending power of $1,200.04 in 2016.

Apparently the big market for this stuff is blog posts, tweets and facebook posts.
Well you now know how much stuff is worth when you read it on facebook!

And farewell to all that!

This morning those lambs remaining from last year's crop were loaded into a trailer and left. They were by and large those who had perhaps not shone in the past. Still when the weather got cold they were considered a bit delicate and whilst the rest stayed outside these were whisked inside and pampered a bit. Having sheep inside brings its own problems.

Wearing a thick woolly jacket they have problems with temperature regulation, they can get too hot, sweaty and can go down with pneumonia and all sorts of other problems. Then because they're on bedding, their feet get soft and overgrown and they go lame. So it's a relief for everybody when they can go back outside as nature (cruel mistress that she is) intended.

We had one who did suffer from its feet. When it came inside we trimmed them because they were a bit overgrown. It seems to have a genetic predisposition to rapid horn growth because I had to trim the feet whilst it was inside and when we put them outside again; I trimmed them for a third time. But it kept hobbling around like an old woman with bunions.

So obviously we kept up the treatment. I would go in with both quad and Sal and I'd catch it. This involved Sal dancing in front of it. The lamb, (about thirty something kilos so we've long passed the cute stage.) would be far too busy keeping an eye on Sal to worry about me and I'd catch it, turn it onto its back and spray its feet with the magical green spray which clears out various infections.

I did this twice and whilst it got rid of the infections, it didn't seem to improve things much. So next time I caught it I put it in the back of the trailer and fetched it home. I then stood it with its feet in a bucket of Zinc sulphate solution. So Sal stared at the sheep, the sheep stared at Sal, and I held the sheep in place for twenty minutes and read a little of 'Three men in a boat,' by Jerome K Jerome. (Highly recommended if you've never read it.)

I then turned the sheep back out with its mates. When I looked at our patient next day it seemed to be much improved. So the following day Sal and I caught it again and gave it another couple of chapters of Jerome K Jerome. Since then it's been walking well; so that's one I can mark down as a success.

But bringing sheep inside always does seem to lead to problems. Ideally lambing ewes stay in for as short a period as possible. Being inside doesn't do sheep any good.

In another life in another world I had to help somebody who was having trouble with their local trading standards department. Apparently the previous winter they'd had a blizzard and lost ten or a dozen fell sheep to the weather. Given there were a couple of thousand sheep in the flock my first thought was that they'd done pretty well, and deserved congratulating on the high calibre of their shepherding.

But their local trading standards department seemed to think that it was cruelty because they hadn't brought the sheep in for winter. So I suggested they got their vet and their breed society to write polite letters to trading standards explaining why you don't house sheep over winter. Indeed if you did, you'd be damned lucky only to lose ten or a dozen.

The letters were obviously written and sent because I got another phone call from the farmer. Apparently trading standards had given up on that approach, instead they were insisting that once it started snowing the farmer should have gone up onto the mountain and brought the sheep down until the snow stopped.

At that point I phoned a few people and discovered that on the day trading standards had demanded a farmer and his children (his only staff) go out onto the mountains to fetch in the sheep, they'd closed their own office as they felt it was too dangerous for their staff to travel to work at sea level! I suggested the farmer point this out, and he heard no more about it.

If you made it up, nobody would believe you.

A gentleman could do no less
Every so often a man must do what a man must do. Or something like that anyway. I was browsing through the books in a charity shop when I became aware of the presence of two ladies. From their comments they were mother and daughter and I'd guess the mother was about my age.

Mother was haranguing daughter because she felt that daughter was going to vote for the 'wrong' political party. Daughter was growing more and more hacked off by this but did remain civil and just squirmed a bit. The mother's monologue was pitched at a volume that indicated that it was in no way intended to be a private conversation, being directed metaphorically over her daughter's head at the entire shop. Have you noticed how the politically incontinent do this?

So I confess I weakened. Now I've shunned electioneering on the web, because it's boring, irritating and an utter waste of everybody's time. But here in the presence of real people I was tempted. So I turned to the mother and asked, in all innocence, a couple of questions that the party whose virtues she was trumpeting was having difficulty answering. Mother shut up briefly and daughter flashed me a smile and gave me a 'thumbs-up'.

Mother relaunched the harangue so of course I just asked a few more innocent questions, when gaps appeared in the flow, mainly because she had stopped for breath.

This discourse continued out into the street and when I turned one way and mother and daughter turned another, daughter gave me another smile and thumbs-up with both hands. Then she went on her way happily whilst mother chuntered about me instead of haranguing her daughter. Surely something I can mark up as a success.

Actually given the length of time I've been exposed to UK politics, it doesn't really matter what the opinions of the mother were and what party she advocated, I'd still have been able to ask embarrassing questions to put her off her stride. Politicians and those who regard politics as a participation sport seem to forget that we, the great unwashed and unlearned, aren't entirely lacking in observational abilities. We don't just sit in a hole eating worms waiting for the wise to open the lid, let a little daylight in, and generously tell us what to think.

So when somebody starts spouting off as how their favoured party, be it Labour/Conservative/Libdem/UKIP (delete as you feel appropriate) has all the answers whilst conversely Labour/Conservative/Libdem/UKIP (delete as you feel appropriate) is the party of the anti-Christ they run into problems. Especially if they do this in the presence of people who've actually lived in the same country for a couple of decades and have a sense of humour. Although in my case I'm hoping to hold out for 'determination to do my Chivalric duty' as opposed to 'sense of humour' or 'being a stirring beggar who just likes winding people up.'

But the whole thing started me thinking, which is always a dangerous situation to get into. There are various bodies, be they charities, political parties or churches which attempt to get our attention and win our support. Now the political parties largely seem to work on the principle that for most of the time they can get by with just hectoring us from afar, just so we don't forget them.

Then when they actually need us they deluge us with junk mail and candidates. The problem with this is that it doesn't seem to work too well. People remember the hectoring as they drop the junk mail into the recycling.

The churches, perhaps because they've been doing it for longer, have tried a wider variety of stances. Yes some harangue you and thrust tracts through the door but don't say hi when they meet you in the street. But the best have picked up on what Christ said about generally helping out and being nice to people.

Now in all candour, being nice to all people, the good, the bad and the politically incontinent, is tough and faced with a lifetime of it; most people would probably accept martyrdom as a preferred alternative. But we can see where in some congregations they find they have individuals who have a gift for dealing with people and a real determination to do something for the homeless, the dying, the prisoners. The successful churches get behind these people, providing them with the support they need to do the work, and those church members who like me find loving my neighbour damned hard work at times can still do our bit to support them and help keep the show on the road.

It reminds me of the quote, "No one after lighting a lamp puts it under a basket, but on a lamp-stand, and it gives light to all in the house. In the same way, let your light shine before others, so that they may see your good works and give glory to your Father in heaven."

Perhaps if our political parties tried to reach out to us through their good works rather than their speeches and promises, then we'd take them more seriously?

But frankly I don't see it catching on. It's not the easiest road to walk. The Christian church has been trying it for the last two thousand years with mixed success.

Oh and back to the real world, we have this blue faced ewe who lambed for the first time last year. It was a nightmare lambing and she had all sorts of problems after it. We weren't even sure if she'd get in lamb this year. Anyway she did but it seems to have taken some doing because she was obviously going to be the last to lamb.

The others finished lambing at least a fortnight ago and our blue faced lady has remained in the pen, accompanied by another ewe who has lambed a while back but has metabolism issues. She was fine, unless the weather suddenly went cold, at which point she collapsed with severe low blood sugar.

Anyway, yesterday the decision was taken that this was getting silly, the blood sugar lady seemed to be sorted so the decision was taken to let them both out, into somewhere handy. We'd just have to hope that our blue faced ewe would be easy to catch and help if there were any problems.

This morning I went out to check sheep and the blue faced lady was there with her two new blue faced lambs, happy as larry and wondering what all the fuss was about.

Sometimes a lady can do no less either.

Dulce et decorum est

This time of year can be difficult for the diligent Border Collie. All these charming lambs scampering about might look delightful but they've got no respect. As old Jess would doubtless have said, if she could be bothered lowering herself to communicating verbally, "If you haven't got respect, you've got nothing."

From the working canine viewpoint lambs are a nightmare. They don't know the rules; they are as likely to walk up to the dog to see what's going on as they are to run away. Then when they do run away they do so apparently at random and at speed.

Added to this, when they're still young, if the dog gets too close, Mum is going to march up and stamp her foot at you. It's not the foot stamping that's the problem; it's the fact that she too is now moving in exactly the opposite direction to that intended, or not moving at all.

Once lambs get to a certain age Mum seems to relinquish her defensive role. Whether she reckons they're big enough or fast enough to look after themselves I don't know.

The other problem is that lambs play. One time we were fetching a mixed batch of ewes and lambs down a lane. One of the lambs (twenty kilos in weight so no longer winningly cute) kept running back the way the flock had come. Nell, who was a properly trained sheepdog, would run after it, turn it, and bring it back. The lamb did this three times, running poor Nell ragged. On the fourth attempt the lamb found old Jess standing in front of it. Jess merely snapped, her teeth meeting so close to the lamb's nose that it must have felt the draught. The lamb stared at Jess, shrugged, turned round and trotted on with the rest. You got the feeling the lamb felt it wasn't fun anymore.

But let's just run through today's simple task 'looking sheep.' First I have to take some feed to the ewes and lambs in the field behind the farm. These are a mixture of the ewes who were the last to lamb (so still need a bit of feed) plus 'pet lambs' who somehow misplaced their mother. Or perhaps their mother misplaced them. Either way they've been bottle reared and are now out on grass but are too small to play with the grown-ups. They also need something to make up for the fact that they're not getting any milk from Mum.

This is easily done, I walk into the field and they come across to see me and I just put the feed down in small piles. Sal, providing as she does, the canine oversight, has nothing to do and just wanders off to one side, nose to the ground, working out what happened last night.

Then I have to take slightly more feed to the rest of the sheep. This means I have to pass through those I've already fed. They're still eating so aren't interested. Except, that is, for two of the oldest 'pet lambs' who immediately abandon the others and follow me. They've worked out that if they look suitably pathetic then I'll give them something out of the bag I'm carrying. These two are both ewe lambs and are being reared with the idea of them joining the flock and having lambs of their own. Because they're hand-reared they'll be a little more domesticated than the rest, which is a mixed blessing. Yes they'll be easy to handle, but because they'll follow when they should be driven and doubtless give cheek to the dog, they can also confuse the rest of the flock. Still I give them a little more feed and go into the next field.

At this point the others see me. So far things have been pretty decorous. I think the sheep in the smaller group have worked out that I'm leaving them plenty. In the big group they're only getting a handful each. They've worked out that the last sheep to Jim isn't going to get anything. So I'm making my way through a surging sea of sheep who frankly don't care. They're banging against me and ricocheting off each other. When you get a really large number of sheep being fed it's not unusual for people to be knocked down. This tends to happen when a ewe moving at speed hits you on the back of the legs at knee height.

Still I keep my feet. Sal watches this from afar. She's going wide, bimbling about out on one flank. Occasionally she'll find a ewe or lamb who is either fast asleep and hasn't noticed my arrival, or alternatively is feeling under the weather and doesn't care. In the latter case you look them over and perhaps come back later with quad and trailer if they need catching and treating.

Then suddenly we have a problem. Sal wandered through a gate and across the bridge assuming I was going that way. But I'm not. So she has to get back through the gate to follow me. Unfortunately there's a mob of ewes standing near the gate watching her suspiciously.

For Sal this presents a problem. A Border Collie has no problems slipping through the bars of the gate. It's just that you don't want to be squirming through them with a rabble of belligerent ewes present. Sal is in a similar position to the young lady in a short shirt, trying to exit the sports car with dignity under the eyes of the drinkers in the pub beer garden. I can see her pondering the situation. Eventually she abandons the idea, makes her way down to the next bridge and wiggles through that gate before catching up with me. Job done, home for the next job.

It shouldn't happen to a dog.

You'll see a lot about how to train dogs to work cattle, but actually you need to give nearly as much time to training the cattle to be worked by dogs. When you stop to think about it, One thousand kilos of bull shouldn't really be all that bothered by ten kilos of dog.

That's where the training comes in. A good dog will quietly do their job without a lot of fuss, gently chivvying the recalcitrant and just keeping things moving in the right direction.

We had a spell where we were dogless for a couple of years. Our dairy cattle rapidly realised this and celebrated this by ignoring me. The cow I was walking behind would walk forward; the others would stop and watch. Effectively unless I was going to bring each animal in individually, something was going to have to change.

So we acquired Boz. Boz was effectively third reserve on another farm because he was no good with sheep. So Boz's owner was almost glad to be rid of him when he discovered I was looking for a dog. So in early middle age, Boz arrived.

He took to us immediately, the moment he discovered that he was 'The' dog. Not only that but his kennel (a disused cattle trailer) was strategically placed so that even when he was fastened up he could see what was happening all the time. Then the big moment came, we had to introduce him to the dairy herd. They were less impressed. Boz didn't do the traditional run round the perimeter bringing them in, instead he just bimbled through them, stopping to sniff this one and in one case to cock his leg up against another. The cows took this badly, shaking their heads, lashing out with back feet and even half charging him. Boz ignored it completely. He didn't apparently dodge, but the lashing hoof came nowhere near him. Once he'd passed through them and knew everybody was awake, he went to the far side of the herd and started moving them in the right direction.

It took him about a week to get them trained. He would walk into the field and it was if cows there saw him, muttered, "Good Grief, Boz is here, is that the time," before looking at their watches and lumbering to their feet. No excitement, no fuss, just Boz quietly getting on with the job.

Sometimes the training has to be done more rapidly. We had a bunch of cattle escape onto our land from a neighbour's farm. We gave them a couple of days to calm down and then Jess and I would get them out of the field and the neighbour and his team were waiting to move them along the road. The cattle, young, feckless, boundlessly fit and just aching for an excuse to run waited for us. Quietly Jess and I got them to the gate and then one of them turned to face back into the field. It started that slow practiced walk that can suddenly turn into a gallop. All the others were watching it with interest. It looked fun. Jess walked straight up to it and stood in front of it. This is unusual; dogs will normally go for the heels and turn the animal. To tackle it head on needs a dog for whom fear is something that happens to others. The heifer stopped and looked down at the dog, reaching out with its nose to sniff Jess. Jess snapped at the nose, her teeth clicking shut the thickness of a piece of tissue paper from it. The heifer stepped back, looked at Jess again, decided that it wasn't going to be fun, and walked out of the gate onto the road. The others followed.

As Jess would say, "If you ain't got respect, you got nothing."

Evaporating Herwicks and other stories.

Sunday morning was a bit hectic. I got my baby 'pet lambs' fed (these are the ones who still get milk) but then had to dash off to church because as well as the normal service we had an extra one. Our village lost two lads in the First World War, and this week was the centenary of the death of one of them. The families had asked if we could do a special memorial service and so we did.

Anyway, walking home from church I got to our yard gate to discover a Herdwick ewe with two lambs standing there. We don't have any Herdwicks. We're far too close to sea level and the grass is too rich and I suspect even the air is too dense. I looked at this outfit with interest. She was a Herdwick but her lambs weren't. Had she lost her own and somebody had fostered these onto her or had she just been bred to a lowland tup?

Anyway I got her and her two lambs in a field with our last three ewes to lamb and the older pet lambs who no longer need milk. I phoned a couple of neighbours to see if anybody was short of a ewe and then went to get a bit of dinner. At about 1:30pm I fed the bunch the Herdwick had joined. She was sitting there quite happily with her two lambs. At 3pm I had to walk through that bunch and discovered the Herdwick wasn't there. She'd gone.

Now that field is stock proof. No sheep have escaped from there in nearly two years now. But then she's a Herdwick. Spring has sprung and they get the urge to head uphill, to where the air is thinner and the grass is coarse. When faced with fences sheep cannot get through, I've come to the conclusion Herdwicks merely evaporate to re-manifest somewhere less convenient.

Animals do get this urge to travel at times. We once had a large black dairy cow calving. She wasn't getting anywhere so I tied her up in the calving box to give her a hand. Anyway after faffing about for a while I decided she needed somebody more competent than me, so I would get the vet. I untied her (just in case she went down when she was untended,) and went to phone. I didn't bother her after that, because given peace and quiet she might have got on with it.

So when the vet arrived we went up to the calving box and discovered she'd gone. She'd jumped over the gate and headed who knows where? It was past 11pm, on a dark (but not stormy) night. So we took a guess on the direction she probably went. There were hoof prints in a gateway where there shouldn't be hoof prints so we went into the field to look for her. Unfortunately we'd just made round baled silage. So the field was full of big black round bales. Driving round in the dark searching for a black cow amongst a lot of black bales is a somewhat surreal experience. Fortunately we found her, got her home and all the movement and bouncing about had been useful. She'd opened up a lot more and the vet had comparatively little trouble getting the calf out. We put her and her calf in a pen with a lot higher gate and left her to get on with the whole motherhood experience.

Consummate professional

Somewhere we have a photo, but it's a real photograph. We think it was taken by a small girl using a disposable camera in a pre-digital age. It has old Boz in the foreground and Jess behind him.

This is what is now called 'succession planning.' Nobody lasts forever, and having been without a dog for a while, we didn't want to go through that again. Not only that, but the current dog helps train the next dog.

Mind you in Boz's case he did teach Jess things, but when it came to working they both had totally different techniques. Boz would bimble quietly through a herd of cows as if soliciting tips or just passing the time of day. Cows would get up and make their way home with Boz wandering about in the middle of them. It was his technique and it seemed to work well enough for him. Mind you I once saw him deal with a cow that refused to get up. Rather than bark at it or get excited, he merely cocked his leg up and piddled on her. It seemed to work as well as anything.

I put some of it down to his breeding. When you looked at him it was obvious that there was more Labrador in his genetics than is absolutely necessary for a working cattle and sheep dog. There again, such are the proclivities of the Labrador that I've been told there are wolf packs deep in Siberia that have never seen man who carry Labrador genetics they've acquired.

Boz seemed to take being good natured to the level of an art form. I remember one winter we had a cow outside with a couple of calves. She was outside because she had problems walking on concrete and we put two calves on her so she didn't have to go through the milking parlour. Every morning I'd take some feed to her, and Boz, as 'the dog', would come with me. To get to the cow we'd have to cross a field with a couple of Shetland ponies wintering in it. One of the ponies took a dislike to Boz and every time we went in the field, the pony would repeatedly charge him.

This was potentially impressive, with head down and thundering hooves. Alas the fact that the pony had a shaggy winter coat making it look like a belligerent pyjama dog rather robbed the scene of drama. Not only that but Boz ignored it. As the pony thundered forward Boz would accelerate very slightly, or slow down just a little, and the Shetland would go galloping past and have to turn round for another go. It might be a small pony, but it had the turning circle of an aircraft carrier!

Another of Boz's quirks was when he was eating. Because at his previous home he'd been fastened up on his own when not working, he never had any fear of anybody stealing his food. So he ate delicately, enjoying every mouthful. Give him a slice of bread and he'd hold it between his paws, nibbling it with evident enjoyment.

Jess on the other hand was 'old school' when it came to moving stock. She went round them in the classic manner and followed behind them making sure everybody was moving at her chosen speed and in her chosen direction. When it came to food, Jess learned early on that whilst Boz might not be worried about anybody stealing his dinner, he seemed to assume that all food put out was his. So Jess soon learned to eat her meal swiftly. As she got older she got more cunning and used to hide it. Indeed this habit never left her. One lambing I was talking to somebody coming out of the lambing shed and they were carrying a dead lamb. They put the lamb down while we talked, then bent to pick it up again. The lamb had disappeared. We discovered that while we were talking, Jess had quietly pushed straw and suchlike over it. She'd completely buried it. She looked most put out when it was found and removed.

Pigs

This isn't really my story, but it's one I thought I ought to share. It concerns a friend of mine so I'll keep things carefully anonymous. Just in case.

A mate of mine worked with pigs early in his career. He then went on to do engineering and become respectable, but at least he started out with his wellies firmly in the muck. The business he worked for was a mainly arable farm, situated on the edge of a commuter village, and the farm just happened to have a pig unit. The owner always reckoned that the system worked well in that when grain prices were low and buyers were looking for excuses to drive them down even more, his arable business just sold the poorer grain to his pig unit. Pigs were far more forgiving than grain buyers with regard to quality. In his more bitter moments he was known to comment that pigs had better conversation and higher ethical standards than most grain buyers as well.

On the pig unit they had a herd of sows for producing young piglets and a finishing unit for fattening the weaned piglets. The whole operation was run sensibly with 'just enough' investment to keep things running properly.

One example of the 'just enough' investment was displayed to the world when it came to moving the newly weaned piglets into the finishing building. Doubtless lesser men, more susceptible to the blandishments of those who sell such things, would have had a race in place.

But here improvisation won out. The arable side of the business produced a lot of straw. This was used to bed the pigs. So when they needed to move the young piglets all that happened was they made a race of straw bales (all small bales back then). Each wall of the race was two bales thick and three tall. A day was spent building the race, and it was taken down over the next week or so as the straw was used for bedding.

The boss would gather his staff, plus a couple of the most sensible lads from the village. (This is where my mate came into the picture as one of said more sensible lads.) They would shut all the yard gates, and then they would, by judicious use of pig boards, gather up the weaned piglets, and quietly and gently walk them down the straw race into the next building. Sadly, on the occasion I'm talking about a rep turned up. He was a big man with a booming voice from one agricultural supply company or another. He drove into the yard, leaving the gate open behind him. He looked round, saw the straw race, leaned over one wall, saw the piglets approaching him and boomed, "Is there anybody about?"

The piglets panicked, the flow backed up as piglets climbed over each other to get away from the terrifying apparition. At some point the straw wall collapsed and suddenly there were piglets everywhere. At this point the rep disappeared never to be seen again. (There were rumours that the pigs had eaten him but they're unlikely to have eaten a Ford Cortina as well.)

For days afterwards, well dressed ladies, some in twinset and pearls, would drive into the yard and hand to whoever was about at the time a piglet. This was normally swathed tightly in a towel to act as both restraint and nappy. The conversation was restricted to, "I found this in my garden/utility room/lounge, and no, I don't want the towel back."

It's a sheep day

You can tell it's on the warm side. Sal has dug herself a shallow depression in the ground to sit in! She's pleased as punch with it now because it's probably a bit damp and cool, but this is Cumbria, in another week it'll be flooded.

So today is a sheep day. Ewes and lambs are gathered in. They were sitting in the shade of hedges, sprawling behind thistles, or alternatively, grazing in the middle of the field with expressions of bland unconcern.

Anyway we fetch them home. The ewes haven't been clipped yet. This is mainly because firstly it was too wet to shear them, then it was too cold to shear them, and then all the shearers were too busy silageing and doing other jobs. But it's entirely possible that the ewes might get sheared this week.

All the time the thermometer is creeping up. When I walk them in, we have one ewe who is panting like an old dog. She's obviously feeling the heat. She quietly stands in the shade when we get to the yard and watches us with casual indifference.

So we weigh the heaviest lambs, there are some ready to go. Then we worm the rest of the lambs, check their feet, put some fly spray on them to deter blowfly and stop them getting infested with maggots. Their mothers will be treated later, after they've been sheared. In a perfect world, once a sheep is sheared there's nowhere for the flies to lay their eggs. Then as the wool starts to grow, you can dip them in something that'll kill all the skin parasites they've got and provide them with some protection for the next few weeks.

It's now distinctly hot, noon arrives and with it both mad dogs and Englishmen retire to the shade with the sheep that we've dealt with, leaving the rest of us out in the sun to get on with it.

And in the middle of all this lot we get two walkers. Ladies with map and compass who are some distance from their chosen path. No, strangely enough it doesn't pass over our silage pit. But still, we direct them the best way to pick up the path they're trying to find and they disappear into the shimmering heat haze. If it gets any hotter, the next party to come this way will be riding camels!

Finally the last sheep are done, we put the flock back out onto grass and they disperse to eat or hide in the shade depending on whim and I'm in to get my dinner.

And somebody tries to interest me in working in London. They must be mad.

Shear bolts, Border Collies and Summer

Every so often something happens and it reminds you of something else, and that reminds you of something else, until before you've finished you're fifty years away and wondering where the time went.

Last night, just before it got dark, I thought I better water some bedding plants somebody has planted. As I stepped outside, Sal, (who currently holds the position of 'working dog') saw me, and sat up, the very picture of Border Collie attentiveness. There was no obvious pleading, there was just a dog portraying efficiency personified. Whatever I was about to do would obviously be done better with her assistance. So I let her out and she supervised the running of the universe whilst I got on with watering the bedding plants.

All dogs are, by definition, dogs, and that is not a dishonourable estate. Some dogs, and a lot of Border Collies, aspire to personhood. They combine being dogs and people. Sal seems to have achieved personhood.

It was her activities earlier in the day that took me back fifty years to our first dog, old Ben.

Ben was technically my dog. Admittedly I was at school a lot so he would accompany my Dad.

When my Dad was still working for my Grandfather, Ben did just that, he accompanied him. Once my Grandfather retired, Ben, without prompting (or more prompting that he'd had previously) threw himself into work. This means that we're talking about the late 1960s here.

Ben wasn't short of eccentric traits, and these entitled him to be regarded as 'The' dog, a person in his own right, and even, 'a character.' He was big for a Border Collie, and as well as working cattle, he also had oversight of tractors and suchlike machinery, feeling it was his responsibility to keep them moving.

One summer afternoon, it might even have been in the much hyped 'summer of love', we were making hay. One person was driving the tractor that pulled the baler; the others were loading the bales onto a trailer pulled by another tractor. And then the baler jammed. This was common enough; too much grass had gone into it and the baler couldn't cope. Only in this case obviously there was too much strain and a shear bolt broke. So the driver would change the shear bolt and the others would drag the hay that was jamming up the works out of the baler. Now all this is caused by a shear bolt doing what it is designed to do, it's the 'fuse', burning out before something more expensive does.

As an aside, there are a lot of shear bolts in agriculture, probably because so much stuff is operating in a difficult environment. Design engineers put them in to help protect the rest of the machine. It's just that I wish they'd give some thought to just where they put them. Almost by definition, shear bolts will be replaced, comparatively regularly, by semi-skilled labour. We had one forage harvester where a shear bolt could only be changed if you lay on the floor underneath it and used spanners to tighten a bolt that was six inches in front of your face. What made this so tricky was that above the bolt was a drive train with several universal joints.

Unfortunately the engineer who designed the drive didn't realise that it was impossible to get a grease gun onto the grease nipples in these universal joints because of all the other stuff around them. So the only way we could keep it lubricated was to pour old oil along the drive train and hope it got in somewhere.

Now then add to this the fact that it's a forage harvester and everywhere fills up with dry grass and dust. Not only that but you've covered large bits of it with old oil, just to ensure everything sticks to it. So when you lie underneath this lot to change the shear bolt, the slightest movement (such as tightening a bolt up) brings another shower of grass, dust and oil down on you.

As the one wearing glasses, I was the obvious person to do that job because less of it got in my eyes.

Anyway I've kept you talking and we can now go back to the baler, where my Dad has changed the shear bolt and the others have got the baler unjammed. Old Ben, as Border Collie on duty, has been sitting quietly watching the whole performance. Finally my Dad starts the tractor. As it starts to move forward, Ben runs in and nips the baler wheel to make sure it keeps going forward, and then proceeds to trot behind it to ensure it doesn't stop again.

And yesterday I remembered this story again. It was another hot summer's day. A hay day if ever there was one. At eight in the morning, Sal and I went out to fetch sheep in. In the interests of efficiency, I rode on the quad, and Sal didn't.

Things were going reasonably well, we gathered the sheep up and moved them toward the gate. Finally the sheep reached the gate and at this point I stopped the quad and shouted to Sal to sit down. I wanted the ewes to see the gate and make their orderly way through it; this they can do better if they don't feel they're being chased.

The problem is that whilst some saw the gate and did go through, the others, deciding that they weren't being chased, just stopped and looked about them in that somewhat supercilious manner sheep have. So I honked the horn on the quad.

To our sheep, the horn is a signal that they're supposed to be moving. Obviously there are times when I drive through sheep in a field because I'm just going somewhere. In those cases, I don't really want the sheep to do anything. So if I'm on the quad and do expect them to move, honking the horn occasionally is a signal to them to keep moving.

As I sat on the stationary quad, honking the horn to keep the ewes moving I heard a noise from behind me. I honked the horn again and this time saw what was going on. Knowing that the noise meant I expected stuff to move, Sal had run in behind the quad and snapped at the mudflaps to get the quad moving along with everybody else.

The tick-box fairy

I was just reading a piece by Sir John Timpson. Somebody had written in saying that he was losing the will to live because of all the box ticking rubbish that came across his desk from compliance officers and others. The wise answer Sir John gave was hire a box ticking officer who did all that crap for the company and let everybody else get on with their real jobs.

To be fair, in agriculture, we get all sorts of utter rubbish poured down upon us from pretty well every inspectorate that can wrangle itself a rural arm. My 'favourite' example of this was the dairy inspector who back in the 1980s insisted that we had a separate 'wash area' in our dairy. We'd never had one because frankly the back kitchen was more easily accessible from our milking parlour than the dairy was. But muppets are not to be denied, and even though he couldn't actually show where the regulations said I had to do this, he was just going to ensure I failed the inspection until I installed one and would charge me £100 a time to do the re-inspection.

So we had our wash area. This consisted of a bucket, with a bar of soap in, and a towel. The bucket was covered in Clingfilm and was placed out of the way on top of the hot water boiler. There it stood, untouched, for ten years, until we gave up milking at which point it was disassembled and was used for something useful.

It's the same as the instruction to wear a plastic apron whilst milking. We had a plastic apron hanging in the dairy. It had been left there by a relief milker who left one on every farm he milked at, so he didn't forget it. I on the other hand never milked wearing a plastic apron in my life, but as the apron hung there in the dairy, another box was ticked.

Still in spite of sundry muppets and other time-wasters life goes on. I went to look sheep this morning. Because it was raining, Sal wasn't sitting outside waiting for me. She appeared when I did, but saw no point in getting wet before it was necessary. We wandered down among the sheep and gave a little bit of cake to the small batch who'd lambed last.

Now yesterday we added to this small batch last year's daughter of a ewe who was in the batch with this year's two lambs. Because all four sheep are distinctively marked you could spot mother, daughter and this year's lambs very easily.

Now if you keep your own replacements you'll regularly stick a daughter back in the same flock as her mum, but in this case we could actually tell who was who. So I've been watching them to see if mum showed any signs of affection to older daughter. The answer is a resounding 'no'. She is 'last year's lamb' and is firmly kept at a distance because 'this year's lambs' take priority. Motherly love is working, but is focussed on those who need it, not those who might feel entitled to exploit it.

Another interesting individual to watch was Sal. A couple of the older lambs tentatively play with her. Various ewes with young lambs disapprove of her entirely and shake their heads and stamp their feet. Generally they treat her with wary respect as becomes one with her dentition.
But, Sal quite likes the taste of the feed I'm putting out for these ewes and lambs. So when I put some on the floor, Sal will drift casually in and eat some. At this point, with noses in the feed, any wary respect goes out of the window and even the smallest and most timid lamb will cheerfully push her away as it tries to eat the nuts Sal is eating.

Oh and finally somebody pointed me to an interesting article. Apparently St. John's College in America, with two campuses in Annapolis and Santa Fe has turned its back on modern fashions in education and is merely doing what universities used to do which is teach students to think. It's an article worth reading, and reminded me of Cash Pickthall, who taught me history back in the Grammar School. He was a great one for using history to make us think.
I remember at the time thinking that if it caught on and everybody started thinking, that would be the end of civilisation as we know it.

Winter fence posts and a tired dog

In an ideal world you'd knock fence posts into the ground in winter or spring. This is because the ground is still wet and is comparatively soft. Not only that but because the ground is soft you can use a fence post with a larger diameter. I admit it'll take more knocking in, but it'll last longer so you might not have to replace it as soon.
Again, in an ideal world, if you have to knock fence posts in during the summer, you'd have a few slimmer ones about. Because, and I'm sure you've worked this one out for yourself, the ground is dry and hard.

Alas, it is not an ideal world. But then you might have noticed this for yourself. So we had a few cattle who tiptoed through the hedge and over the fence on the other side. Before I put them back in the right field I had to string up a breast wire, and that meant I had to hammer some posts in. Sixteen of them, and even with a steel bar to make a preparatory hole, it was harder work than it really needed to be.

So with the fence fixed, the cattle had to be collected from the next field, taken down onto the lane, along the lane and back into the field they should have been in. A simple enough task.

But cattle are more individualistic than sheep, and faster moving. Luckily I was on a quad, and Sal is a dog who can cheerfully run at 30km per hour, looking back over her shoulder to see if you're keeping up. (She really shouldn't, one time she ran into an elderly ewe and they both looked remarkably put out by it all.)

But we started the cattle moving, and between us, Sal and I sort of kept them in a group, and sort of kept them moving in the same direction. Then the inevitable happened, one decided not to play. She just put her head down and ran in a direction of her own choosing. Jess, who knew her trade, might have spotted the errant bovine about to start its mad career, and if she got chance, would have restored order by a sharp snap to the nose. But by the time Sal had realised what was happening, the heifer was off.

So Sal and I set off after it. Sal managed to get ahead of it and turn it, and then it started running in a different direction. Again Sal and I set off after it. This is where the quad shows its mettle. It doesn't get tired and you can just pull quietly ahead of the running animal. Eventually the heifer decided that it wasn't as much fun as she thought it was going to be and turned back to her mates. Sal and I followed her back to the rest of them, got them out of the gate and they thundered along the road and into the proper field. Job done.

We got home and normally Sal will stand somewhere in the middle of the yard with an expectant expression. This is the expression of a dog who rather hopes something else interesting is going to happen.

On this occasion she just flopped down next to the cattle trailer that serves as her kennel with a little sigh, and watched me put the quad away with a look of relief.

Given the amount of running she'd just been doing, I can see her point.

The little ones are the real problem

We were moving some heifers; they'd escaped from field A into field B. I fixed the fence and two of us, plus dog and quad went to bring them down field B, along the road and back into field A. This went well enough except for one of them who took umbrage at the presence of the dog and jumped out of field B, over two perfectly good fences and a bit of broken down hedge, into field C.

We looked at her disappearing down field C to join stock already present, shrugged and decided to get the rest moved to field A. We'd let her calm down a bit and move her tomorrow (or whenever.)

That evening I checked field C. Our errant heifer wasn't there. So I wandered round a bit and finally discovered she'd worked her way through two perfectly stock-proof hedges to rejoin her mates in field A, entirely of her own volition.

Moving cattle is easy if everybody keeps calm. The problem is that young cattle quite like to run. There's obvious something atavistic about it all. The thunder of hooves, the dust, the endless prairie, all they need is John Wayne. As an aside here I always remember my Grandfather's comment,

"Hell I wish I'd had John Wayne working for me."

"Why Grandad?"

"Because he's just driven Longhorns into a canyon and they've come out the other end Herefords."

But anyway, a big part of moving cattle is keeping it boring. Not only that but it helps if they know you. So every day, I, and whoever was 'the Dog' would walk through every batch of cattle we had. Indeed I'd often take a little bit of feed with me. When I mean 'a little bit,' I'm talking a couple of pounds for a batch of sixty or so. It reminds them that you're one of nature's nice people and worth following in case you might spontaneously produce more of the stuff for them.

I've regularly moved thirty cows with their calves at foot just by walking among them with the bag, then out of the gate and along the lane with Jess quietly trotting along at the back making sure the laggards kept up. If she'd been able to close gates behind us, it would even have saved me having to go back to do that later. All this happened in Jess's earlier career when she had proper cattle to play with and wasn't reduced to putting fear of Dog into sheep for a living.

But when you're dealing with cows and calves, the problem isn't the cow, it's the calf. The cows are, in a vague sort of way, rational. When they set off at a run you can normally pinpoint the stimuli which provoked it. With calves they can just do it for no reason whatsoever.

The problem with calves running is not only that they are fast, but they're not really bothered about directions or destinations, but are concentrating entirely on the running. So they can blunder through fences, end up in ditches and generally cause all sorts of problems. Not only that but as the dog tries to turn them they can run straight over her, or alternatively, they might stop abruptly, tentatively sniff the dog's nose and then run wildly in an entirely different direction.

Once they start running, the only real solution is to put Mum back in the field, let her restore order and then bring Mum and calf out together.

Then you have the problem of gateways. Twenty of them will troop quietly through the gateway with no trouble, and one calf will somehow miss the gap and stand facing the hedge bawling for Mum. And Mum is standing on the far side of the hedge bawling back. Something like the calf shouting;-

"Help, help, I'm lost, I'm trapped, I'm alone in the world, doomed, doomed."

And from the other side of the hedge, "So help me, don't you make me come in there or you'll be sorry."

"Doomed, doomed, there's no way out, help."

"You wait 'til your father gets home, we'll see what he has to say about it."

At the same time the dog is standing there muttering, "I can see why they eat grass, everything else is smarter than they are."

So the solution to this problem is for a human to very quietly edge the calf along the hedge until it can see the gate again. If you're lucky the calf will move slowly, a few steps at a time, and finally inspiration will strike and it'll follow the others. If you're unlucky it will set off at speed in some random direction and you'll have to start the process all over again.

Bigger than Brexit? Unesco awards Lake District World Heritage site status.

Every so often something comes along and initially you wonder whether it'll make any difference. And then it occurs to you that it might be wise to read the fine print. So you heroically refuse to allow umpteen pages of dense bureaucratic prose to put you off and you start reading. As you read you slowly come to realise that the world has changed around you and that nothing can be the same again.

You might or might not have noticed that Unesco has awarded the Lake District World Heritage site status. If you want to read their document it's at

http://whc.unesco.org/archive/2017/whc17-41com-inf8B1-en.pdf

The people I feel sorry for are the various groups of environmentalists who have been trying to drive sheep from the fells and who have been pursuing their own, often conflicting, environmental agendas. They got what they asked for and perhaps they are now wishing that they hadn't asked.

What is the most important thing in the Lake District? What holds it all together, keeps it the beautiful place everybody wants to visit? Which body should step forward to accept the grateful plaudits of the masses?
Here I quote Unesco

"ICOMOS generally concurs with the view of the State Party but highlights that the maintenance of the English Lake District's visual qualities is highly dependent on the sustainability of some 200 shepherding farm families and their herds of "hefted" Herdwick sheep. The system has to face crucial challenges of shifts in global markets, changing agricultural subsidies and schemes, particularly given the exit from the European Union, introduced diseases, and climate change."

Yes, the whole thing depends on 200 farming families who're working long hours for very limited financial recompense. In fact I doubt any of them will earn anywhere near as much as the National Trust Agents and National Park officers who spend so much time telling them what they can and cannot do.
Not only that but for the last couple of decades we've had the same endless refrain, get the sheep off the hills, cut down numbers. As Unesco says

"In the past, overgrazing and other farming management practices threatened the environmental and natural values of the property. Although these practices have been corrected, there seems to be a certain imbalance in the consideration of the natural values favoured over the cultural values of farming practices. In the future, measures should be adopted that consider also the cultural values and benefits of the farming activities."

Basically think of Unesco as the school teacher who's standing in front of a bunch of big kids (various conservation bodies) and jabbing her finger at them, telling them that they've got to stop bullying the little guys. But let's just stop a minute and think about this. Government has accepted this. If it's true for the Lake District, then it's true for most of our countryside. We've got ourselves a good general principle worthy of wide acceptance here.

"In the future, measures should be adopted that consider also the cultural values and benefits of the farming activities."

That I should live to see the day!

Another issue we have is that for most Cumbrians, tourism is more of a blight than an economic opportunity. The Lake District has about 40,000 inhabitants. The area gets about 20,000,000 visitors a year. That's 15,000,000 day visits and 4,000,000 overnight stays.
Just to put that in context I was talking to one Lake District farmer from Langdale. On one May day Bank holiday the Park did a survey of the number of people walking though his lambing fields (while their sheep were lambing) and walking up to Stickle Tarn. The flow of people averaged 1135 per hour thought the day. That's what tourism means for the people who are doing the work that maintains the Lake District as people like it.
Fortunately Unesco can see the issue here and has an answer

"ICOMOS recommends that mechanisms are set up to ensure that economic benefits from tourism are increasingly shared also with shepherds and farmers, recognizing the important ecosystem and management services they provide in maintaining the landscape."

Well fancy that, the peasantry getting a cut of the income stream that only exists because of their work over the centuries. Damned commie pinko stuff this I tell you!

But it isn't just about the 200 farming families. The Lake District works because it's a community (or at least that bit that isn't all second homes). The whole community needs help. Especially when we're getting floods which block all the roads due to extreme weather events. Unesco is on the ball as always.

"The management system should be expanded to develop strategies that prevent depopulation, including affordable housing, neighbourhood shops and promotion of local products, strengthen the disaster risk strategies and incorporate into them local knowledge, and develop interpretive plans based on the Outstanding Universal Value of the property so as to assist visitors' understanding."

Yes you read it here; we are now to have affordable homes and building within the National Park! If I'd written that last year you'd have assumed I'd been smoking something illegal. Finally there are the additional recommendations. I'm just including them all.

ICOMOS recommends that the State Party gives consideration to the following:

a) Providing assurances that quarrying activities within the property will be progressively downsized and extraction volumes limited to what is needed for carrying out conservation of the assets supporting the attributes of the property,

b) Formally committing to avoiding any negative impact on the Outstanding Universal Value and related attributes of the property from the NWCC energy transportation facility being currently planned; and informing the World Heritage Centre about the results of the Heritage Impact Assessment, and how these will be integrated into the planning consent and in the development consent order (DCO),

c) Informing about the timeframe of the integration of World Heritage consideration into the local plans and policies,

d) Developing proactive strategies, including alternative national farm-supporting policies, with the farming community, to address the issues that threaten the viability of the shepherding tradition that maintains many of the landscape's significant attributes; recognising and financially compensating farmers for their heritage services in caring for the cultural landscape, as well as values such as genetic diversity of herds and food security,

e) Rebalancing programs and funding dedicated to improving natural resources with the need to conserve the valuable cultural landscape that the Lake District is by acting on its key attributes and factors,

f) Strengthening risk preparedness strategies for floods and other disasters that incorporate local knowledge on how to cope with recurrent disastrous natural events,

g) Developing convincing programs to prevent depopulation, including:

a) develop affordable housing for new households and for local retirees,

b) ensure that communities have a mix of commercial outlets that serve the local community,

c) further develop and market local products that benefit residents and local farmers,

h) Developing an interpretation strategy at the landscape level which communicates the different strands of the Outstanding Universal Value by using the documents put together for the nomination dossier,

i) Ensuring that careful attention is paid to conservation of landscape-defining features such as land-use patterns, structures such as shelters, dry stone walls, hedgerows, and also to vernacular architecture and Victorian buildings, not only in designated Conservation Areas, but in the whole property,

j) Submit by 1st December 2018 a report on the implementation of the above recommendations to the World Heritage Centre and to ICOMOS;

Not only that but they cannot just kick this one into the long grass as far too embarrassing to deal with. Teacher expects their homework back in for marking by the 1st December 2018 or there'll be trouble.

Already the howls are coming up from the vested interests, the liberal commentators and those who earn serious money from writing about conservation. If you want to read a rant of monumental proportions which verges on the hysterical at times, I'd recommend one by George Monbiot where you catch him in full flow. Thanks to UNESCO the writing is now on the wall and a lot of the conservationists don't like what they're reading.

Making a hash of it man!

The problem is that if you are a farmer, it sort of sticks with you. You don't stop being one just because you're asleep, on holiday, or reading Facebook. Anyway I saw a post of a friend's Facebook page saying how much money would be generated in the economy if we legalised marijuana. So of course I just had to sit down to do the maths, but from the farmer's point of view.

It's interesting trying to get any decent economic figures. First I tried to look for how much marijuana the average user uses (by weight). It's the sort of thing you need to measure the size of your market. Now there are a lot of figures quoted but people tend to quote the proportion of the population who use the stuff or the estimated financial value of stuff seized.

What I did discover was that the average joint apparently contains 0.32gms

Not only that, but apparently the average US user smokes 123 joints per year

So it's possible to estimate the size of the market, but what about output?

Apparently you can get 500gms per plant growing outdoors

The trouble with a lot of articles about growing marijuana is that they regard individual plants as precious. On an agricultural scale you wouldn't be worried about yield per plant; you'd be worried about yield per acre.

Looking for a comparison, if I was planting industrial hemp then it's common to use 10cm spacings between rows. So there you could be looking at about 300 plants per square meter. Obviously growing for marijuana you might sow for a lower crop density. Perhaps aiming at 30 plants a square meter.

But here I'm just guessing, because whilst 30 plants per square meter might optimise marijuana output per plant, at 300 plants per square meter you might still get as much marijuana, but also a valuable fibre crop as well.

But let's stick with 30 plants per square meter.

First, assuming that each plant only produces half the marijuana it does when being cosseted inside, that's 30 x 250gms which is 7.5kg per square meter. In marketing terms, that's 23,438 joints.

All in all this is enough to last 190 average consumers the full year.

Now the Home Office produced figures which show that 2.1 million people in the UK use the stuff. Now obviously they won't all smoke the full 123 joints a year. But if it's legal others might try it and users might smoke more. So let's have all 2.1 million people smoking 123 joints. So the estimated market is 258,300,000 joints which needs 11020 square meters to grow on. This is just over a hectare, not quite three acres.

Even if I'm an order of magnitude out, or even two orders of magnitudes out, we're only talking about somewhere between three and three hundred acres.

Legalise marijuana in the UK and I suspect in 10 years, it'll just be part of the fibre hemp industry. Growers will be planting varieties which will produce fibre and marijuana and if Tesco and Asda are willing to pay a reasonable price for the marijuana then more will go for processing. As for price, it's suddenly an agricultural commodity; it'll be so cheap that in some years farmers will plough it back in because it's not worth harvesting.

But then we get VAT and excise duty. At the moment three quarters of the price of a bottle of cheap whisky goes to the government. The various consumer taxes on legal marijuana could be the money tree our political parties are looking for.

Sometimes it rains a bit

Last week it was our local agricultural show, North Lonsdale. Occasionally we have a glorious day for it, because in an infinite universe, anything is possible. But frankly I reckon we have more damp, or at least gloomy days than we have sunny ones.

Still last week you have to admit nobody was going to accuse the day of being half-hearted about it. If you want a day to sum up the Cumbria summer, it was the one. It started by blowing a gale and accompanied this with driving rain, yet by midafternoon it was actually quite a nice day and the mud was thickening nicely.

I arrived on the show field at about 7:30am because I was going to help with ACTion with Communities in Cumbria with their stand. By 9am, in spite of the driving rain, we had not merely erected a gazebo; we'd taken it down again before it left of its own accord.

But still we found a new home in one of the tents. A fair few traders hadn't turned up. Now to be fair to them I can understand that. We had some leaflets to hand out. In the morning we left them in the car, there was no point at all in thrusting paper into somebody's hand. It was turning to papier-mâché even as they struggled to read it. A trader could lose thousands of pounds in damaged stock without selling a thing.

But anyway in the tent we made ourselves at home. In passing I'll say a big thank-you to Ulverston Auction Mart and the local NFU office for keeping us supplied with coffee. Facing those conditions inadequately caffeinated is a recipe for disaster.

But once underway we did all sorts of things. We talked to people about disaster planning. Given the weather people could see where we were coming from with that one.

Also we did a survey, you know the sort of thing. I showed them a list of services rural areas need and asked "Which of the following services are most important to you as a rural dweller?"

At one point you could even do the survey on line. Alas but that lacks the ambiance enjoyed by those for whom it was a part of the full North Lonsdale show experience. But if you fancied I suppose you can always fill your Wellingtons with tepid water before sitting down at the computer to tackle the questionnaire.

After about noon the sun started to come out and people appeared. These were the ones who were there to support 'their show' because they know these things are important. Not only that but when we got them doing the survey we'd see them wandering off in their small parties still discussing whether affordable housing or broadband was more important. We didn't merely ask questions, we started a discussion and people went away thinking. I suspect we were the most subversive organisation on the show field. If everybody started thinking then that would be the end of civilisation as we know it.

And as with all these shows, there were any number of high points. Wringing the water out of my cap for the third time wasn't really one of them. Still for me, one of them was coming across one chap who I drafted into answering the questions. Once you got him talking you discovered he was a young man with a real heart for the rural community and the problems we have.

Then there were the half dozen or so young lads, aged about ten, who drifted into the tent. With infinite mud and no adult supervision they were having a ball. But in the tent they didn't splash mud around, answered the questions, and came up with some good points.

Like the lad who said they'd like more parks and footpaths. I was about to say 'but you've got the countryside, what more do you want; but then I realised. He was a decent lad and just wanted to know where he could go. I was born round here and at his age knew everybody.

So I could go anywhere. But since then the links between the various parts of the community have broken down, he doesn't know who owns what, he doesn't know who to ask. It's something to think about and hopefully do something about.

And then there were the other traders, to pick one out I'd say a big hello to the shy self-effacing chap from the Damned Fine Cheese Company.

Their Black Gold is absolutely beautiful. So beautiful that I've been forced to break off from writing to cut myself a slice.

Another to mention is local author Gill Jepson. Gill claims to have been at school with me, but all I can say is that she must have lied about her age to get in early. It takes real nerve to carry books through the driving rain, even if you're going to sell them in a big tent, but Gill did it.

So yes, it was a bit wet, but it was a good day.

Timing

They always say that timing is the secret of good comedy, and frankly it's the secret of success in agriculture as well. I knew two chaps who retired after a lifetime in dairy farming. For a tenant, selling your dairy herd basically pays for the house you have to buy.

The two men were much of an age; their herds were pretty much the same. Yet the first got an average of £1,100 a cow, the other chap who retired two years later averaged about £600 a cow.

Why the difference? A mixture of things, most of which wouldn't even make the papers, politicians tweaking EU dairy policy, supermarkets cementing their dominance in UK milk sales, there were currency fluctuations, all sorts of things.

But what it meant was that one chap had £66,000 to show for a life-time's work, the other had £36,000.

I know another chap who kept farming for a few extra years in an attempt to build up a bit more capital. He worked out that because of those five years, with dairy cow prices falling and the EU decision to end milk quota leading to a collapse in the price, he'd effectively knocked £30,000 a year off his capital for the privilege of working the extra five years.

Obviously there are swings and roundabouts. I came to the conclusion that we managed to survive the whole EU quota scheme without gaining or losing on it. Some people who retired and sold their quota when it was at its height did OK. Still, no matter how good you are at the job, whether you get out of the job with a home and a decent pension is pretty much blind luck.

It's one reason why I'm watching the Brexit negotiations with no real sense of panic. We're still at the posturing stage.

Take the Northern Ireland border issue. How on earth can you decide what sort of border is needed until you have agreed what sort of trade agreement there is between the EU and UK. If I was Theresa May I'd just offer the Irish Republic free-trade and promise them that as long as they stay out of the Schengen agreement there won't be a border.

As for the insistence that the European Court of Justice should deal with matters regarding EU citizens in the UK after we leave, frankly it's a nonsense. I'd love to see what the Canadians would say if the EU insisted on it as part of the terms of a trade deal. The EU cannot expect any sovereign state to agree to it.

But at some point the posturing will have to stop and then they'll have to agree something. I very much doubt that they'll manage to achieve an agreement before the two years is up. Given the structure of the EU they probably couldn't get all member states to sign up to a deal in that period. So far we've seen the Spanish threaten to veto any agreement that doesn't solve what they see as the Gibraltar problem, whilst the latest thing I heard was the Greeks want the Elgin marbles back as the price for their agreement. It'll take more than two years for the

Commission to negotiate the agreement with the member states.
So we'll 'crash out'.
Probably, but don't let the hysteria worry you. Nothing is ever as good as they promise and nothing is ever as bad as they threaten it will be.
Take the Brexit vote as an example, instead of the collapse of civilisation we were promised, Cumbria has done quite well. A low pound has boosted tourism and pushed the sheep price up nicely. I know somebody who started their flock last autumn and is selling their first lamb crop this year and is doing quite. This sort of boost can get a business on its feet.

But why am I not worrying about Brexit? Well in the last thirty years I've had EU/UK Government ;-

Retrospectively impose milk quotas
Inflict their management of two major FMD outbreaks on us
We had the BSE fiasco
We had the fiasco that was the single farm payment system
We've seen Bovine TB go from being a minor problem in a few parishes to being endemic across vast swathes of the country

If I had been in the wrong place at the wrong time, any one of those could have screwed us financially. For example during BSE outbreak there were more farmer/butcher suicides than there were people who died of the disease.

If I was the sort of person who took it personally I might claim that pretty well twice a decade the EU/UK Government has done its best to leave me homeless. Brexit? Yeah well, whatever. It's only governments; don't confuse it with real life.

'Honest to God' and her ilk.

One thing you don't see on farms much now are the various van salesmen. They'd travel from farm to farm selling stuff. The vast majority of it was at least quazi-legally acquired.

You'd get the 'gate salesmen' who'd turn up with an open pickup loaded with metal gates. Sometimes they'd got a load cheap, perhaps picked up at a bankruptcy sale; sometimes they'd picked up some cheap steel and had a mate who could weld. Some of the latter gates could be good value, especially if they'd picked up some decent steel angle-bar cheap. At least with angle-bar you can see the thickness of the metal you're buying. Gates made out of welded steel tubes take a lot more sussing out. I've seen tubing used where galvanizing the damned stuff probably doubled its weight!

Then there were the chaps selling clothes. They would pick up seconds from the Lancashire mills or stock clearance from shops closing down and they'd stack it all in the truck and head out. I remember as late as the 1980s one lad proudly presented for our inspection a dozen boxes of shirts he'd found, still in their wrappers, when he'd bought out the entire stock of an old clothes shop. They were the old style, with separate collars which were attached by studs. Far more importantly they were so long that when you wore them, you were sitting on them when you sat down. Men had a damned sight fewer back problems brought on by working in a cold draught when they wore shirts like that.

Then there were the tool sellers, the purveyors of carpets and rugs, canned foods where the labels had suffered in storage, honey in five gallon drums, patent medicines for people or for livestock, and any number of others. They worked on the principle that they acquired it cheap and sold it for whatever mark-up they could get.

I suppose there isn't the market any more. In 1950 there were 196,000 dairy farms in the UK, now there might still be over 10,000. The number of other farms types of farm has also declined. Not only that but with less than a third of the manpower in farming compared to what there was in the 1960s, people are just too damned busy. On top of this, when some bright spark comes into your yard to quote you a price, it's the job of a moment to ask google for a price comparison.

Also I suspect that people are now so busy and so stressed that they're more willing to tell a time wasting salesman to leave; normally using a two word expressing ending in 'Off', the first word having between four and six letters. What you have to remember is that whilst some of these traders you saw once and then never again, some were fixtures, you'd see them most years. They'd built a market for themselves, their stuff was OK, the prices were OK, and they were good enough to deal with. Not only that but by definition, it was all delivered to the yard.

Most of them have sort of faded from memory now, there's a couple I might recognise if I bumped into them somewhere. Yet there's one I'm never likely to forget. I haven't a clue what her name was but if I went onto any farm in South Cumbria or North Lancashire and asked if 'Honest to God' had been recently they'd know exactly who I meant.

She (and it was a she) was unusual in that I don't remember many other women selling gates. She had her husband with her, but he said nothing, he merely lifted gates off and on the pickup. (He seemed to have taken his role from watching Fanny Cradock and her husband Johnnie.) I don't remember her starting a sentence with anything but 'Honest to God......' Trust me; she started a lot of sentences. But to be fair to her, she certainly saved you the trouble of starting your own. It was a conversation that verged on the monologue. I think her sales technique was just to overwhelm you with a constant barrage of spiel until you bought something if only to get rid of her.

It once took us over an hour to get rid of her, we were obviously too courteous; far too courteous because she kept reappearing every year. Finally she turned up on a day when my parents were both away. I was, by definition, at least twice as busy as I normally was and drove down the yard with the tractor going flat out to find her and her husband standing by their truck looking for a victim.

She flagged me down and shouted something.

I replied, "I cannot hear you for the tractor."

She shouted something else, longer this time.

I replied, "I've got to keep the tractor at full rev. I cannot let it stop."

This was perfectly true, if the tractor wasn't at full rev there was a chance I might have heard her, and be blowed if I was going to stop it and waste half an afternoon.

She shouted something else, perhaps it was more eloquent this time, I don't know, it might even have been beseeching.

I replied, "Sorry, cannot hear you, have to go, needs fixing."

With that I drove off round the corner in among the buildings. I left the tractor running full rev until I saw her and her husband drive out of the yard.

They came back one more time but we were lucky, we saw them coming and managed to disappear.

The dog does not entirely approve.

At the moment Sal is barking. She doesn't bark a lot, only at times when she feels she ought to be out there sorting things out in her own inimitable way. As Border Collies go she has two foibles. The first is that she doesn't like sheep standing close to the hedge. Over the years, when we've been looking sheep, she's noticed that we occasionally have to walk across and disentangle on that has managed to get itself caught up in briars. Or perhaps it's stuck its head through the wire netting and cannot pull it back out.

So when she sees a sheep too close to the hedge, she'll run across and move it. At times this can be quite useful. I've seen lambs get themselves tangled and just sit there, convinced they're completely stuck. The arrival of Sal suddenly galvanises them into action and, quite literally, 'with one bound they're free.'

Her other foible arises from the fact that she lives in a cattle trailer. Sometimes in it, sometimes under it, sometimes sleeping in the snug and sheltered plastic drum within the trailer; it all depends on what she particularly wants to do. All this is perfectly normal for the working collie. What gets her barking is that from her cattle trailer she can see one end of a field we know as 'The Meadow.' Her foible is that she objects to sheep grazing on that bit of the field and seems to regard it as a personal affront. It must be admitted that the sheep seem to take no notice at all of her barking.

We're not sure why she finds their presence so irritating, perhaps it's just the deeply held conviction that sheep without a Border Collie in close attendance are going to get into trouble? Whether she was brought up on 'Little Boy Blue' with 'the sheep in the meadow, the cows in the corn' I wouldn't like to speculate.

Now her attitude isn't a 'problem' as such, she doesn't bark interminably at them. Just lets us know they're there, in case we come to our senses and do what she considers the obvious thing and let her out to supervise them.

Over the past few days there have been more sheep wandering onto the bit of the Meadow she can see. Basically every year some of the older ewes have to be culled, and you fetch in some younger sheep. Some you might breed yourself, but a lot of people will fetch in new blood as well.

What's been interesting is the way the batches have or have not been mixing. Firstly there was a batch purchased from somebody who was retiring. We stuck them in with a small group of our own sheep and for the first few days the two batches largely kept separate, although the two batches might graze close to each other.

Then three more groups were purchased at a sale. Now each group came from a different farm. So each of these three groups tended to stick together but shunned the other four groups. They didn't stick with the main batch because it wasn't 'their flock'. In an attempt to keep out of the way of 'not their flock' the little clusters of like-minded sheep push out to the edge of the grazing area and thus graze the patch of ground Sal can see and feels protective about.

Anyway today they were all fetched in and the new arrivals were treated for worms, liver fluke and suchlike, then they were all let out back into the field. Having been stirred up and mixed I noticed that the little groups are far less exclusive.

Cattle can be like that. If you have one batch of cattle grazing a big enough area, and let another lot onto the same ground, the two groups can retain their cohesion for quite a while. We've put a second group onto a field and a couple of days later, because circumstances have changed; we've taken the first group out. The groups hadn't mixed and our moving one lot didn't bother the other lot in the slightest. But again, if you bring two lots together in the yard and let them run down the lane together into the field, the self-imposed barriers between the two groups seem to disappear remarkably quickly.

Social scientists might draw conclusions from this but if I were them I'd be wary. If their tinkering with the underlying fabric of reality leads to Border Collies disapproval, I predict that things will not go well.

Keeping the show on the road

My Dad entered the job market in the 1930s, which wasn't perhaps the best time, all things considered. Not only that but given his background he had a choice between going down the mines as an iron ore miner, or farm work, and being the rebel he was, he chose farm work. The wages were far lower, the hours longer, but when you were injured in an industrial accident it was at least above ground.

His first half year, when he was fourteen, earned him the princely sum of £13, plus of course his board. It's reassuring to know that the great British public have always been careful to ensure those working in food production aren't lured from the straight and narrow by too much easy money.

But before he started working full time, while he was still at school, he would work for the father of a lad he was at school with. Effectively he made sure he had learned the basics of his trade before he went out to start convincing people to pay him.

His mate's father had a small farm, so they were never going to make a lot of money. On the other hand, one advantage of a small farm is that you cannot lose a lot of money either. Grow a thousand acres of wheat and lose £100 an acre, you've lost a £100,000. Grow ten acres of wheat and lose £150 an acre because you don't have the economies of scale, you've still only lost £1500.

But back then we're talking much smaller amounts of money, a farm worker 'living in' did well to earn £2 a week. But my dad always had an admiration for his mate's father. He had a good eye for horses. Not fancy horses, or racehorses or anything like that, he was good with your ordinary work horse. So whilst he farmed in much the same way as everybody around him, he'd keep his eyes open for those working horses that were broken down with hard work.

The delivery horses going round town, those owned by companies and used by employees who weren't perhaps as committed to the horse as an owner-driver might be. He'd give the horse a good looking over first and then he'd buy them at sales or even straight from the company.

Then he'd just let them out into a field with his own working horses and leave them for a while. After a few months he'd harness them up again and start them working a little but nothing strenuous. Then when they were fit and strong again he'd sell them on. Apparently one of his best deals cost him perhaps ten shillings and year later he sold it for £11. But that was the way farmers got through the Great Depression.

There are a lot of tricks like that which have survived, farmers who've spotted a niche and have quietly filled it. The best niches are the unfashionable ones which are profitable enough to be worth doing but not so profitable that they tempt others to try and exploit them.

A while back I was chatting to one old farmer who had just sold some remarkably elderly ewes with lambs at foot in the spring sales. He'd also learned his trade from his father who'd learned his in the 1920s and 30s. They'd always bought a few pens of cull ewes when everybody was getting rid of them and the price was rock bottom. They'd worm them, stick them out on some coastal marsh that they had and leave them there to get heavier or whatever. Unbeknown to him, the previous winter a tup had got in with his collection of old ladies and just when he was about to start selling them fat, they'd started lambing. So he lambed them and sold them with lambs at foot. Given he probably paid a tenner a head he was happy enough to take seventy or eighty pounds for a very elderly ewe with two lambs. His pride and joy was a small ewe with her single lamb who made £60. He'd never actually bought her.

She'd come through the ring when he was buying the others. She'd looked so small and pathetic that the vendor couldn't get a bid for her. So the frustrated vendor had surreptitiously dumped her in with a batch that had already been sold and had quietly disappeared.

Autumnal

With dawn on the 1st September, autumn struck. I went out to look sheep and whilst it was bright, it was cold. The mist was just burning off from our moss land and the dew was very heavy on the grass. Half an hour later the sun was up high enough to feel warm, but there's no longer the power in it there was even a week or so ago.

Next day was so glorious, after checking sheep I just kept going, walking for most of the day. A roe deer was lurking among the rushes and the dog missed seeing it. I saw it when it moved. In the distance, silhouetted against a very blue sky a hawk was hovering, trying to hunt. But all the time it was being harassed by small songbirds and finally gave up and left. By the time I got there the hedgerow was alive with chaffinches with no sign of a hawk.

Round here, harvest still isn't finished. This isn't unusual, it's not uncommon for us to have an August where we just get bands of rain and showers coming in off the Atlantic, whilst at the same time much of the UK seems to be stuck in a continental weather system meaning they stay hot and dry (or in winter, cold and dry.)

The problem with harvest this late in the season is that dawn leaves everything so damp so that the weaker September sun takes until afternoon to get grain dry enough to combine.

On the other hand, it's been a green year. Our grass has grown well. Normally in August things can start looking a bit brown and parched but this year we've stayed deep green right the way through. Given that so far the gales have held off, everything has still got a lot of leaves on it and the hedges also look well with the trees in their many differing shades of green.

On my way home I fell in with a chap walking his milk cows back for afternoon milking. They gave the impression of being entirely content; plenty of grass, the sun on their backs, no flies to bother them at this point of the season, and heading home for milking. They just ambled happily along, occasionally stopping to grab a mouthful of grass from the road side. It's the sort of day where even the dog appears happy to just let things happen at pretty much their own pace.

OK so today it was chucking it down when I was out checking sheep, and the first thing I did when I got home was throw everything I was wearing into the washing machine and put on something else, but the rain still isn't particularly cold.

Culture isn't cheap

Earlier this week I was at a conference about 'cultural' and 'natural' landscapes. Throughout the conference we got references to how important agriculture was in creating these landscapes. Indeed Unesco in their granting World Heritage Site status to the Lake District pay generous tribute to the two hundred sheep farming families whose activities largely created the landscape everybody but George Monbiot loves.

For me the underlying problems were highlighted by a gentleman whose name I never caught who is involved in the Solway Plain AONB in North Cumbria. He complained that part of the plan to safeguard the cultural and natural landscape was the grazing of dairy cows. But in the last few years the grazing cattle have been moved inside all the year round and the grassland has been cropped rather than grazed. This had brought changes to fences and hedges (because they are no longer worth maintaining) and to plant varieties in the grassland.

There wasn't time in the conference to unpick this, but I think it is actually an excellent example of how little real money is going into supporting the environment.

If you assume a 200 acre dairy farm producing 1.5 million litres, then they're probably getting £12,000 a year single farm payment as general support, and I suppose that if they're very very lucky they might get as much again for pushing the aims of the AONB. So let's assume £24,000. (This is very much the top of the range for that sort of farm.)

In the last few years for many dairy farmers the milk price dropped from 30p per litre to between 14p and 15p per litre. This means that the farm income has fallen by between £210,000 and £225,000 a year. This sort of income drop can mean bankruptcy. To put things into perspective we saw farming families going into Christmas with the bank overdraft at the limit, all family credit cards maxed out, and they hadn't paid a bill for two or three months. They were surviving on 'trade credit.' Basically a lot of agricultural supply companies bit the bullet, pushed up their own overdrafts, and became lenders of last resort for these people. The companies were just hoping that the prices would pick up before everybody, including them, went bust.

While you could point to 'market failure', it was a decision by government (EU) to stop managing the market which made this failure possible. The sole beneficiaries have been the major retailers who have just pocketed the extra margins they made on milk.

In reality you cannot blame the retailers. Their shareholders, many of them pension funds and similar, need large amounts of money. These funds are under pressure because of changing rules due to the financial crisis and people living longer so demanding more money from their pensions.

But going back to the Solway plain, what do people actually want? If they want an environment managed by grazing cattle then they'll have to pay for grazing cattle.

There's three ways they can pay for it. The first is through prices. Just to give ourselves a sense of proportion; by some measures, after the Second World War, people in the UK spent 40% of their income on food. Now it's between 10% and 13%. When I first milked cows there were about 100,000 dairy farmers in the UK, now there are about 13,000. When you've got 100,000 people being supported on the land, then they can do things like trim and lay hedges properly and do all the other labour intensive tasks. When you've got 13,000 being supported by the land, something has to give.

But when you stop to think about it, what happened to the money once spent on food? Well how much do you pay for your mobile phone contract, your internet connection, your netflix subscription? (Just to give three examples of things which weren't even concepts back then.)
To a fair extent a lot of money has poured into companies like Amazon, Google, Facebook etc. As an aside it isn't just food, think how cheap clothing has become. Now, rather than pay somebody a living wage to produce clothing in the UK, you can buy garments produced by somebody on another continent working for a pittance.
So if food prices went up, a lot of industries would just collapse because the consumer wouldn't have the disposable income to spend on them.

The second way is to subsidise farmers to produce the goods. The problem is that this means the state has to step in and fill the gap between what the market has provided and what the family needs to survive. I know farming families that run a business turning over half a million pounds a year. But at the end of the year the family earn less than their eldest daughter who's just started working as a teacher.

the state would have to do is step in and fill the gap. When milk is 30p per litre at the farm gate there might not be a gap. When the price crashes to 14p per litre then the state might have to find a quarter of a million pounds per business to keep the sort of agriculture they wanted. Otherwise farming would evolve to become a system that could survive at 14p per litre.

Ironically before we went into the EU we had a 'deficiency payments' system which effectively did this. There was an annual Price Review where it was decided by government what price was necessary, and then a deficiency payment was made to cover the gap between the guaranteed price and the real price. Obviously if prices were higher than the 'guaranteed price', nothing was paid. When we joined the EU this system had to be abandoned for the far more expensive CAP.

The disadvantage of this system from the point of view of the environment is that the Treasury (and the tax payer) would probably rather fund the sort of agriculture we can have at 14pence per litre than the sort of agriculture we could have at 30 pence per litre.

Finally the state (or some quango) could just step in and run the land directly. This is inevitably going to be a far more expensive option in that you're unlikely to get state employees who are willing to work 4,500 hours a year for less than the minimum wage.

Big skies and ice-cream

I remember a friend of mine once asking me if I was impressed with the 'big skies' of Cambridgeshire. We were visiting the area at the time and given the area is pretty flat, I suppose you can have quite a lot of sky. What she hadn't realised was I live on the edge of Morecambe Bay. Our horizon is at least forty miles away in most directions. We do 'big skies' better than most.

Anyway today the weather was 'fine enough' so I decided I was going for a walk to enjoy these skies. A friend was heading north and could drop me off not far from Pennington so I followed a lot of quiet lanes and came into Ulverston from the north. I walked through town, picked up a pie and a coffee and then headed south.

My plan was to hit the coast at Bardsea and follow it almost home. This meant I could visit one of the Nation's premier catering establishments. Roy's Quality Ices.

If you've never dropped off and got an ice-cream from Roy you don't know what you're missing. I've lost count of the sheer number of homemade flavours they have. Today I treated myself to a double cone with orange and chocolate chip on one side and plum and damson on the other.

From then on it's a case of just following the coast. For the first couple of miles you follow a trail between beds of reeds and the shoreline proper. Then you come to the 'flat rocks.' These are beds of limestone. At this point the rushes have largely gone and when I was a child and swimming there, the rocks ran into the sand and the tide washed up onto them. Now the beach is shifting and there's grass between the rocks and the sea.

After the flat rocks you come to Baycliff. From here on, if the tide is out I leave the shore and just walk straight across the sands. If you set your sights on Piel Castle and walk dead straight for about four miles you'll not go far wrong.

It's a different world out there, at times the coast road is hidden and the only noise is the splash of your feet on wet sand and the shout of seabirds. Another sound you can sometimes hear is the distant roar of the tide coming in. This afternoon it was far too far out for me to hear it.

The only 'problem' is that there are two becks come down to the shore and of course they have to make their way out to join the sea, wherever it's got to. When the tide is in, the waves wash round their outfalls. When the tide is out the two becks wind their way out towards deep water.

Their channels probably take four or five miles to cover three miles. Given the amount of rain we've had this summer, and especially in the last few days, there's more water in these channels than there normally is.

Tackling them is 'fun.' You either tackle them well out to sea where they've started spreading and aren't too deep, or you tackle them closer to the shore where they've somehow broken themselves into several minor channels with stone bottoms and are comparatively easy to cross. It's the bit in the middle where the various minor channels have reunited that's the tricky area. The other problem is that when you're further out and they've spread, you can suddenly find yourself crossing 'cow belly' sand. Just keep moving! Don't stand there wondering what's happening. It's a relatively firm form of 'quick sand'. (More of a moderately paced sand really.) All in all, survivors probably cross the channels comparatively close to the shore.

Another advantage of the 'big skies' is that you can see the weather coming. This morning the forecaster had muttered vaguely about there being sunny periods with showers between 3pm and 4pm. (Forecasters do this a lot with regard our area. We do sunny periods and scattered showers remarkably often. As far as I can tell, if the driving rain relents briefly, and the sun flickers momentarily through a small gap in the clouds before the rain restarts, any weather forecaster worth their salt will book that down as sunny periods and scattered showers.)

But anyway, with my usual excellent timing we had them predicted for when I was out on the sands with no shelter, ideally placed to have any rain driven straight onto me. But I could see the clouds moving across, and it soon became obvious that I was walking across the front of their advance. So I just kept moving and inadvertently avoided them all.

So there you have it. There cannot be many other walks in the UK where the guide tells you to take a bearing and walk dead straight for the next hour or so.

I would have mentioned it before but I've been busy

Apparently in this age of social media, where we're all on-line all the time, it's impossible to be out of touch. So if the theory's right I have no excuse for getting back to you earlier.

But in this beautiful area we are truly blessed. You see, mobile connection is distinctly iffy. My phone, an elderly battered nokia, (which cost me £20 of which £10 was phone credit) lives switched off for 90% of the time. If you've not got my personal number don't let it worry you. When I'm at home there is no signal so the phone lives switched off. When I'm out and about working, the phone doesn't accompany me because on those few occasions where I won't be out of signal, I'm busy so don't want to be bothered with a phone. Finally if I'm in areas where there is signal, I'm either driving, in a meeting, or merely walking quietly from a to b and happy with my own thoughts. So obviously there is no place for a phone.

But I'm pondering upgrading my phone. The Sellotape holding the nokia together is still sound, but apparently it's one of the first generation to offer colour. Which means you cannot actually read their screen in direct sunlight; which is a bit of a sod if you're scrolling down looking for a number to phone. Not only that but without my reading glasses I couldn't read it anyway.

So I drifted aimlessly round various suppliers looking for a phone. I wanted a decent camera, wifi (because when the computer is down we've no way to get our email) and a pay as you go contract.

To be fair, some of the sales staff could cope with this. There was only one who was convinced that I should sign up for a £12 a month contract, even though I pointed out that after the first ten months I'd have been better off having just paid cash for the phone.

I did try explaining, again, that on pay as you go my phone normally costs me less than £10 a year. But you know what it's like, the lights were on but there was obviously nobody in. As a previous generation of journalists used to say, "I made my excuses and left."

So don't expect anything to happen on this front any time soon. But I might have actually got a new phone by this time next year; or then again, perhaps not?

Still I've also been busy. Real life and real work has intervened. Ewes are going out with the tup and everything has to be got ready. The ewes have already been vaccinated, but then we had to get them in, dag them out (cutting away mucky wool from the rear end) treat them for worms, lice and fluke, and finally give them a dose of multivitamins just to make sure there were no hidden deficiencies were weren't aware of.

Then the tups were wormed and got a good dollop of bright coloured raddle smeared on their chests so we can tell if they're working or not. Broadcasting your love-life in glorious Technicolor is obviously the way to go.

Don't look at me, I'm not an engineer

I genuinely haven't a clue how much of my life has been spent working with, and on, drum muck spreaders. The idea is simple; a long drive shaft spins, powered by the tractor. Fastened to the shaft are flails, steel chains with a solid block on the far end. So when you've filled the spreader, you just drive out into the field and start the central shaft rotating. The flails spin round and smash up the muck in the drum and throw it out in a reasonably even covering.

Over the years I've changed the bearings at either end of the shaft. I've changed bearings and tightened drive chains in the system which connects the tractor power take off to the central shaft, and I've shortened the flail chains.

What people who've never used these don't realise is spinning them round as quickly as we do, the chains slowly stretch, and this means that eventually the steel blocks on the end of the flails start hitting the drum. The drum can only take so much of this so basically you've got to shorten the chains.

Now there's a proper way to do it. The central shaft has a series of brackets welded to it, and a bolt goes through the bracket and also through the last link of the flail chain. So you unfasten the bolt, remove the chain, cut off the last link, and rebolt the shorter chain back into place.

Life being what it is, the process isn't quite as simple as that. Firstly the whole thing has been marinated in muck for a year or so. It's probable that the bolts are rusted solid. Not only that but when you get them out you discover that some of them have worn a bit with the flails pulling on them, so while you've got them out it might be time to replace them with a new bolt because you'll probably never get them back in. This time, grease your new bolt well before you fasten the nut in the vague hope that next time you'll be able to undo it. (You won't but greasing it will give you the warm smug glow of somebody who's thinking ahead.)

So rather than this being a job you can do with two spanners, what you really need is an angle grinder for cutting the nuts off, a hammer and punch for getting the bolts out. Then you can use the angle grinder to cut the bottom link off. Then open your pack of new bolts and put one of them in.

Unless of course, you're just way too busy. You see, you're on your own, (Lone working is my life) and you've got perhaps an hour at most to work on this job before you have to start afternoon milking. Tomorrow morning, you'll be using the spreader again, so that hour is all you have. Under these circumstances you might be tempted to try a different method.

With the angle grinder cut through the chain link that is bolted to the shaft. Don't worry, it's so jammed with muck and rust it's not going to move. Remove the rest of the chain, shorten it, and then put the end back through the cut you just made. With a hammer, bring the ends of the cut link closer together and just weld the gap shut so the flail chain is now in place.

Now do the next one.

I remember one time wondering how much of my life has been taken up with keeping knackered machinery working using techniques that aren't in the manual, and whether, one day, I might ever be able to afford a piece of new kit that wasn't held together by muck, rust, string and hasty welding jobs.

But here at the scruffy end of agriculture, worrying about how to cope with too much newness has never been an issue to be honest.

Once you've dealt with a water leak in a galvanised metal pipe by covering the leak with weld, whilst water is still running at low pressure through the pipe, very little upsets you anymore.

Apple Chutney and Refrigeration Engineers

Way back, probably in the late 1960s, the Milk Marketing Board decided to try and move farmers away from putting their milk in churns for collection and shift over to bulk collection. It would save the MMB a fortune in labour and suchlike. Also the MMB paid for the churns, farmers had to install their own refrigerated tanks.

But they offered a small premium if you shifted to bulk collection. I think it paid for the tank over three or so years, and so we made the leap and bought a 150 gallon bulk tank.

I can still remember it being delivered. The driver appeared in our yard with his articulated lorry. He'd got to where our lane met the main road; glanced at the map and realised he wasn't sure whether he could turn round when he got to us. Not only that, but there were no mobile phones so he couldn't ask. So he'd backed his lorry about three-quarters of a mile, down a winding single-track road, between tall hedges, with at least one right-angled bend.

This was a seriously impressive feat of driving and my dad commented on it. The old chap just smiled quietly and commented that after spending the war driving Scammell Tank Transporters, anything else was pretty much a doddle.

Time went on and in the late 1970s we ended up getting a bigger tank, 300 gallons this time. This was delivered by a chap who was an owner/driver who got all those complicated jobs employees don't want. So he'd set out from home, load up with milk tanks and travel up one side of the country and down the other side, delivering them. He was normally home after three or four days. To pad his week out, on the other days he'd deliver ammonium nitrate fertiliser in hundredweight bags.

His next door neighbour was a fanatical gardener and asked if he could buy some ammonium nitrate. The driver said he'd have a word with a customer, and managed to buy a full bag off a farmer for him. He warned his neighbour to be careful with it, because it's not the diluted stuff you buy in garden centres. Next morning, as he set off to collect a lorry load of milk tanks, he noticed that his neighbour had put the ammonium nitrate on his lawn. He'd put so much on it looked like there'd been heavy hail, the lawn was white. A bag, which would do a third of an acre perfectly happily, was largely used on a lawn not much bigger than a double bed.

When the driver arrived home three days later, the lawn was black. Anyway he advised his neighbour not to do anything; he probably hadn't killed the lawn.

He hadn't, and the following summer he had to mow it every other evening or else it would have got totally out of hand on him.

But drivers aside, we were now left with pretty complex refrigeration equipment, compressors and suchlike. Of course it goes wrong. It'd been installed by a chap the MMB recommended at the time so we'd contact him for servicing and suchlike. He was based in the Lancaster/Morecambe area. Anyway you could never get hold of him and finally we got hold of a firm in Penrith. They send an engineer down and he sorted things out. We mentioned the other company and the engineer just laughed. Apparently if you wanted to get hold of them you had to phone the right pub. The chap was apparently a legend within the industry; he'd serviced the freezers in a cinema somewhere and ended up with melted ice-cream running through the foyer.

So we stuck with this chap from Penrith until he retired. He'd learned his trade in Glasgow and when he first started he'd get to various jobs around the city by climbing onto the tram or bus with his toolbox and letting public transport take the strain. Obviously that isn't an approach that is ever going to work in Cumbria.

But the reason this chap came to mind is apple chutney. My mother used to make apple chutney occasionally, because in all candour we can have a lot of apples. But the problem with cooking apple chutney is the smell of it permeates the entire house, often for days. Anyway this chap was having a bit of supper with us after finishing working on our tank, and when the conversation turned by chance to chutney, he announced he had a method of making chutney without cooking.

My mother got the recipe off him and made some and frankly, it was a success. Anyway to scroll down through the years, I'm faced with a lot of apples. I like chutney. In fact I've always been partial to cold meat with a bit of pickle. So I decided to make some apple chutney.

Could I find my mother's recipe? Not a hope. It was written on a piece of A4 lined paper over forty years ago. But anyway, we have google. So I had a look at various recipes and decided on this one.

450g apples, peeled and cored
225g onions, quartered
225g stoned dates
225g sultanas
225g Demerara sugar
1 small teaspoon   ground ginger
1 small teaspoon   salt
cayenne pepper, to taste
225ml white wine vinegar

Chop the apples, onions and dates. Put the mixture into a large bowl and add the sultanas, sugar, ginger, salt, cayenne and white wine vinegar.
Leave for 36 hours, stirring occasionally, and then put into warm sterilised jars. It keeps for months, if not years.

I'm at the 'stirring occasionally' stage at the moment. It's looking interesting. I used large crab apples and added a little more sugar. I'm quite looking forward to it.

[Just to comment that it was actually rather good and I highly recommend it]

Linguistic good taste.

I took the car in to get an MOT and service this morning. As I walked home two women passed me walking in the opposite direction. As one said to the other, "He were having a fag behind the recycling bins."

Such is the joy of the English language that this probably means something entirely different depending on what part of the English speaking world you hail from.

Apparently it was the Canadian, James D. Nicoll, who commented that "We don't just borrow words; on occasion, English has pursued other languages down alleyways to beat them unconscious and rifle their pockets for new vocabulary."

When we acquire these words, we sometimes give them meanings that the original owners had never contemplated. So we have raddle. This can apparently be spelled ruddle or reddle (because all three words mean the same thing).They may have originated as a term meaning 'to paint red.'

About the only use for raddle now is when you smear it on the chest of a tup or ram before turning him out with his harem. It has the advantage that it rubs off on them and you know that he's working and that they're coming in season.

Obviously a ewe that has been smeared with raddle is 'raddled' and that's another word that has wandered off into more mainstream parlance. I suspect that it's not perhaps as widely used as it might once have been.

It's funny that dyes of varying sorts seem to linger around the fringes of agriculture. Years ago (probably pre-EEC) there used to be 'stockfeed potatoes.' What happened was that when the potato price collapsed, the government would buy up surplus potatoes that weren't needed, to put a bottom in the market. They'd then have them sprayed with a purple dye and sold cheaply to farmers for livestock feed.

Because the supermarkets and other retailers didn't particularly want the very big potatoes, they were often the ones chosen for cattle potatoes. Given that they were both very large and very cheap, I remember a lot of talk about the number of chip shops where you might find purple stained potato peel in the waste bins. After all the dye didn't soak into the potato, and it also had to be safe because livestock were going to eat it.

Another place where they use a lot of dye is the slaughterhouse. Because of various regulations, some offals cannot be eaten. To make sure they're kept out of the food chain, government inspectors will watch as they're sprayed with dye. This stuff is designed not to wash off, to ensure that the stuff sprayed goes for proper disposal. To be fair to the authorities, it works.

There are disadvantages. I remember taking cattle in, and one of the lasses was doing the paperwork for me in the office. One of the slaughtermen came in off the line and handed her a sheaf of papers. She examined them carefully and then gingerly took them off him. Because the lads were spraying the dye about, they'd get it on themselves and then it'd get on the paperwork, and then it'd get everywhere.

As she said, "It gets so that I have to really scrub my hands before I go to the loo. Otherwise my husband keeps asking me whose are the hand prints on my knickers."

Noises off

With farming life you get seasonal sights and scents, but you also get seasonal sounds. I remember stopping the tractor on top of the silage pit where I was buckraking grass. I sat there and listened and could hear seven forage harvesters working on seven different farms. Since then, four of those farms are no longer in existence, the houses are domestic dwellings and the land is farmed by neighbours.

Mind you, round here the neighbours are still family farms. If you wander into the yard looking for somebody, the boss is probably the one with a muck fork and wheelbarrow, not somebody in the office playing Solitaire on the computer waiting for the broadband to come back on.

This morning as I walked round checking sheep, the seasonal sound was the maize harvest. In my lifetime I've seen breeders produce hardier varieties of maize and a crop which was once rare in the south of England can now be seen growing regularly in Ayrshire. Because October was such a sodden month round here, I suspect that the harvest is running slightly late. As it is, this far north we can only grow maize for cattle feed, and the sound is the noise of the contractor's big self-propelled forage harvester working away.

It has to be said that modern farm machinery looks awfully expensive. I remember seeing figures which said in the 1960s you had to sell 3,000 finished lambs to buy the average tractor. Currently it's about 10,000 lambs to buy the equivalent mid-range tractor.

So a lot of us use contractors. For the maize harvest the contractor will turn up on the farm with over half a million pounds worth of equipment. The tractors will work all year round, the loading shovel might spend winter loading salt in a local authority distribution depot, whilst the self-propelled harvesters will start with silage at the beginning of May and finish with maize in November (or December if it's a bad year.)

I must admit I'm not a fan of maize. I've got nothing against it as a crop or a feed, but I'm not enthused by the season you have to harvest it in. I remember one year when people round here were still trying to harvest it between Christmas and New Year. In this area, milk cows will go inside for the winter in October, and I'm old fashioned enough to get nervous if all their winter feed isn't inside with them. Having to rely for winter survival on a crop that isn't harvested and might never be doesn't make for a good night's sleep.

In this area, cattle tend to spend winters inside. It's not that they cannot cope with the weather, more that round here our winters are so wet that the land cannot cope with cattle. It is possible to winter them outside happily enough, if there aren't many of them, you're feeding them on a stubble field you are going to plough anyway, and they've got plenty of room to lay down on dry ground with a bit of shelter from a hedge.

Sheep on the other hand are a lot lighter on their feet. Not only that but they don't take well to being housed. I remember years ago talking to somebody who did house his ewes. He used to bring them in and shear them again. If he left them with the wool on they'd sweat, get chilled and get pneumonia.

So with sheep at this time of year we're constantly managing the grass. Grass will grow if the soil temperature is over 4 degrees C, but at that point it's growing pretty slowly. So at some point the grass will probably 'run out.' Also at some point in the next few weeks, our bottom land will get so wet that even sheep would make a mess, so we have to take them off it. So at the moment we're trying to get the bottom land eaten off before we have to abandon it for the winter.

Yet because the tups are in with them and we're hoping to get the ewes in-lamb, our ewes also need a 'rising plane of nutrition.' At the very least they don't want to go short. So we cannot 'eat off' that bottom land too enthusiastically. Also we're already hoping to get them off the lambing fields. This means that these fields get a chance to green up and have a bit of grass on them for when ewes start lambing.

At some point we'll have to start carrying hay or silage out to feed our sheep. Later, when they're heavily in lamb we'll have to take a concentrate feed out to them. But the more grass they've got, the less expensive feed we have to buy. So managing the grass is something you've got to get right.

Getting the timing right

It's interesting watching the effect that changing the clocks has on livestock. With dairy cows they adjusted very rapidly. If you were an hour 'late' they were all queuing in the cubicle house muttering to each other, wondering where you'd got to. If you were an hour early they were all sitting snoozing in their cubicles. They'd turn their heads to give you a surprised look, wondering what on earth had got into you. But by next milking they'd completely readjusted their internal clocks.

Sheep on the other hand pass through life with a blithe disregard for the time. You appear, you do whatever you're doing and you leave. As much as possible they ignore you. It's only when you start feeding them in winter that cupboard love kicks in and they keep an ear cocked for your arrival. Even then it's not the time; it's the sound of the vehicle which they react to.

Sal, current Border Collie, resident guardian of good order, and for all I know, Keeper of the Sacred Flame of Eribor, has her own innate sense of timing and refuses to be swayed by the clock.

She will appear outside her kennel at what she considers the right time. There she can glance in through the windows and check whether I'm having my breakfast or not. She is reasonably generous; she's willing to give me a quarter of an hour or so. Finally she feels that the day is wasting, she obviously has things to do even if the rest of us haven't. At this point she will bark to remind us that time is passing. The fact that thanks to the clock changing I appear an hour later is an almost personal affront.

It should be noted that her enthusiasm for starting work is weather dependent. When the rain is drifting in sheets across the yard, she obviously catches up on her reading or whatever, because she manages to stay snug and out of sight.

Anyway this morning was pleasant, so Sal was chivvying me along well before I'd finished my coffee. As we walked down to the Mosses to check the sheep down there, there was rag on the grass for the first time. Whilst I was down there I had a look at the hedge I was working on last winter. It was so overgrown I had to quarry it rather than merely lay it. Sal was mooching about in the undergrowth deciding how the next bit ought to be tackled.

It was one of those quiet mornings. The wind turbines spun languidly, energy generation was something that happened elsewhere. At one point I could hear a leaf as it fell, tumbling through the branches on its way to the ground. The twenty-first century was a dull rumble barely at the edge of hearing.

Who is this Jim Webster anyway?

Well I've farmed in South Cumbria all my life, milked cows for thirty years, run a suckler herd and reared calves. Then life went and afflicted me with sheep.

As well as that I've been a free-lance journalist, mainly covering agricultural issues, as well as being the CLA's national livestock adviser for about ten years.

I've also had four fantasy novels published in paperback and innumerable novellas of a similar length to this short collection of stories

To round this off I've got a wife and three daughters, and in spite of this, no dress sense whatsoever.

I've never been able to keep a diary, but over recent years I've written a blog. This is just a collection of blog posts.

The easy way to find out what I've written is to go to my Amazon page, https://www.amazon.co.uk/l/B009UT450I

Printed in Great Britain
by Amazon